STUDY SKILLS FUN!
GAME KIT & CD

95 Classroom or Small-Group Activities That Promote Positive Study Habits

By
Marianne B. Vandawalker

For Grades K-6

D1075333

ABOUT THE AUTHOR

Marianne B. Vandawalker is a former elementary school counselor from North Carolina. She has presented workshops at various state counseling conferences and is the co-founder of KalMar Workshops. Marianne is the author of several best-selling activity books including the *Character Fun Game Kit.*

10-DIGIT ISBN: 1-57543-178-5
13-DIGIT ISBN: 978-1-57543-178-9

REVISED/REPRINTED 2010
COPYRIGHT © 2003 MAR∗CO PRODUCTS, INC.
PUBLISHED BY MAR∗CO PRODUCTS, INC.
1443 Old York Road
Warminster, PA 18974
1-800-448-2197
www.marcoproducts.com

Leader's guide and CD-rom graphics from: www.shutterstock.com
Reproducible game card graphics from: www.clipart.com

PERMISSION TO REPRODUCE: The purchaser may reproduce the activity sheets, free and without special permission, for participant use for a particular group or class. Reproduction of these materials for an entire school system is forbidden.

ALL RIGHTS RESERVED. Except as provided above, no part of this book may be reproduced or transmitted in whole or in part in any form or by any means, electronic or mechanical, including photocopying, recording, or by any information storage or retrieval system without permission in writing by the publisher.

PRINTED IN THE U.S.A.

CONTENTS

PART 1: LISTENING STUDY SKILLS

PART 2: ORGANIZING, MANAGING TIME, POSITIVE WORK HABITS, AND GOAL-SETTING STUDY SKILLS

REPRODUCIBLES INCLUDED ON CD
(Inside Back Cover)

Silly Putty Directions
Name The Object Drawing Cards
Built It & They Will Come Cards
Name That Word Cards
Dot-To-Dot Pictures
Willie McGurgle Poem
Creation Word Cards
Get-Together Game Cards
Happy Traveler Story
Treasure Hunt Cards
Listening Action Stories
Quiet Kelly • Little Invisible Alien • The String Puppet
The Visiting Martian • What's Behind Grandma's Rocker?
The Winner • Quiet, Cozy Town • The Heroes
Twisted Listening
Pay Attention Mind Cards
Pay Attention Ear Cards
Pay Attention Eyes Cards
Pay Attention Body Cards
$100 and $500 Dollar Bills
Listening Cover-Up Words
Listening Cover-Up Cards (Fire)
Listening Cover-Up Cards (Water)
Listening Cover-Up Cards (Ground)
Listening Cover-Up Cards (Sky)
Beach Party Cookout
Hamburger Parts
A+ Bop Cards
Schooltime Statements
Hop To It Questions
What Time Is It When… Cards
Balloon-Landing Questions
Hit Cards
Studying Horse Feathers Statements
Studying Horse Feathers Circles
Roadblock Cards
Shape Up! Tickets
Fold & Check
Dodge City Incomplete Sentences
Key To The City Cards
Hole-In-One Cards

PART
1

LISTENING STUDY SKILLS

INTRODUCTION TO LISTENING SKILLS

Even though listening encompasses most areas of learning and is an essential part of emotional growth and intellectual development, this important skill is rarely taught in today's classrooms.

Good listening skills help students improve their cognitive and emotional competencies. Having good listening skills improves a person's ability to gather information, build trust with others who feel the person is paying attention to what they are saying, develop a cooperative spirit, and learn to empathize with others. On the other hand, poor listening skills make learning difficult and can destroy relationships and communication with others.

Good listening skills play a major role in developing emotional intelligence. Combined with such relationship skills as empathy for others, nonverbal communication, and conflict management, listening skills build self-awareness and awareness of others.

Since developing and using good listening skills is crucial to many important aspects of a person's life, classroom time and direct instruction must be given to this on-going developmental skill. This emphasis will bring students to a crucial level of listening, thinking, responding, and participating in their own learning, thereby helping them control impulsive behaviors.

Specific listening-skill practice requires students not only to listen with their ears but also to observe with their eyes, interpret body language, and reflect with their minds by responding and remembering. Specific listening-skill practice also involves responding correctly to the message given.

HOW TO USE LISTENING MATERIALS

The Action Listening and Focusing Skill Activities in this book have been used in kindergarten through 6th-grade classrooms. They have also been used successfully with:

- special education students with learning disabilities
- special needs students with trainable ability
- ADD and ADHD students
- hearing-impaired students who learn to focus on the interpreter and expand their ability to use sign language.

The Action Listening and Focusing Skill Activities also provide opportunities to work on social-skill development behaviors such as taking turns, communicating with others, and using good manners.

The Action Listening and Focusing Skill Activities and Listening Action Stories are also effective in small groups. The Listening Action Stories can also be used in very large groups.

Many of the Active Listening Activities have been around for many years. Including them in this program increases the likelihood that they will be readily available to everyone.

ASCA STANDARDS FOR PART 1

ACADEMIC DEVELOPMENT

Standard A: Students will acquire the attitudes, knowledge and skills that contribute to effective learning in school and across the life span.

A:A1   Improve Academic Self-concept
A:A1.2   Display a positive interest in learning
A:A1.5   Identify attitudes and behaviors that lead to successful learning
A:A2   Acquire Skills for Improving Learning
A:A2.2   Demonstrate how effort and persistence positively affect learning
A:A2.4   Apply knowledge and learning styles to positively influence school performance
A:A3   Achieve School Success
A:A3.1   Take responsibility for their actions
A:A3.2   Demonstrate the ability to work independently, as well as the ability to work cooperatively with other students
A:A3.5   Share knowledge

Standard B: Students will complete school with the academic preparation essential to choose from a wide range of substantial post- secondary options, including college.

A:B1   Improve Learning
A:B1.2   Learn and apply critical-thinking skills
A:B1.3   Apply the study skills necessary for academic success at each level
A:B1.6   Use knowledge of learning styles to positively influence school performance
A:B1.7   Become a self-directed and independent learner
A:B2   Plan To Achieve Goals
A:B2.3   Develop and implement annual plan of study to maximize academic ability and achievement

CAREER DEVELOPMENT

Standard A: Students will acquire the skills to investigate the world of work in relation to knowledge of self and to make informed career decisions.

C:A1   Develop Career Awareness
C:A1.4   Learn how to interact and work cooperatively in teams

PERSONAL/SOCIAL DEVELOPMENT

Standard A: Students will acquire the knowledge, attitudes and interpersonal skills to help them understand and respect self and others.

PS:A1   Acquire Self-Knowledge
PS:A1.6   Distinguish between appropriate and inappropriate behavior
PS:A1.8   Understand the need for self-control and how to practice it
PS:A1.9   Demonstrate cooperative behavior in groups
PS:A2   Acquire Interpersonal Skills
PS:A2.6   Use effective communications skills
PS:A2.7   Know that communication involves speaking, listening and nonverbal behavior

Standard B: Students will make decisions, set goals and take necessary action to achieve goals.

PS:B1   Self-Knowledge Application
PS:B1.2   Understand consequences of decisions and choices

ASCA standards for pages 7 and 41 are from: American School Counselor Association (2004). ASCA National Standards for Students. Alexandria, VA: © 2004 by the American School Counselor Association

BE A BEARY GOOD LISTENER
INTRODUCTION ACTIVITY TO GOOD LISTENING

GRADE LEVEL: K-5

PURPOSE: To help students learn to use the whole body for good listening and begin to establish rules and expectations for good listening

OBJECTIVE: To demonstrate and practice good listening by teaching elementary-age students to use parts of the body as good listening tools

MATERIALS: ☐ Large stuffed, jointed bear

PRE-LESSON PREPARATION: None

PROCEDURE:

Tell the students:

This is (<u>NAME OF BEAR</u>). I want you to look at this bear and think about all the different parts of its body that are needed for good listening. Each time a part is named, we will take time to tell why the part of the body you chose is important. Who can point to a part of the bear's body that you think is very important for good listening?

Hand the bear to a student volunteering an answer and have him/her point to and identify the chosen body part. After the body part is named, the leader should elicit the information mentioned below while the student holds the bear, moving it to appropriate positions when certain questions are asked. The body parts need not be chosen in the order presented below. After each part is discussed, ask for a volunteer to name a different body part that is needed for good listening and pass the bear to the student volunteering the answer. Continue the activity until all of the body parts mentioned below have been identified and discussed.

EARS—Ask the students the following questions, allowing time for answers after each.

- What are the important sounds in class?
- Which sounds in class are not so important?
- What helps the bear listen to the important sounds in class?

- As you listen in class, why do you need to concentrate on the important sounds such as the teacher's directions and not on what your friend is telling you?
- Can the bear listen with its ears if its head is looking in the desk or resting on it? Why or why not? (Student may have the bear look in or lie down on a desk.)

EYES—Ask the students the following questions, allowing time for answers after each.

- Where does the bear need to focus its eyes when the teacher is giving directions? (Student may have the bear look at the teacher.)
- Where does the bear need to focus its eyes when it is doing class work? (Student may have the bear look at classwork.)
- Where should the bear look if a classmate is called on to answer a question? (Student may have the bear look at a classmate.)
- What will the teacher think if the bear is looking away during listening time?

NOSE—Ask the students the following questions, allowing time for answers after each.

- Where does the bear need to point its nose when the teacher is talking? (Student may have the bear point its nose toward the teacher.)
- What will happen if the bear points its nose toward the window? (Student may have the bear point its nose toward the window.)
- What will happen if the bear points its nose toward a friend? (Student may have the bear point its nose toward a friend.)
- What will happen if the bear points its nose toward the inside of its desk? (Student may have the bear point its nose toward the inside of its desk.)

MOUTH—Ask the students the following questions, allowing time for answers after each.

- What is the bear's mouth doing when it is listening to the teacher?
- What happens if the bear is talking while the teacher is talking?

BRAIN—Ask the students the following questions, allowing time for answers after each.

- What helps the bear's mind concentrate on what is being said in class?
- How will asking questions or answering the teacher's questions help the bear's brain listen better?
- How can the bear keep itself from being distracted during a discussion or while the teacher is giving instructions?

HANDS/PAWS—Ask the students the following questions, allowing time for answers after each.

- What are the bear's paws doing when the bear is using good listening skills? (Student may have the bear sit with its paws in its lap.)
- What happens if the bear's paws are holding something the bear can play with?

- Where will the bear's eyes be looking if there is something in its paws? (Student may have the bear look at its paws.)

HEART—Ask the students the following question, allowing time for answers.

- What will happen if the bear does not want, with all of its heart, to listen to the teacher?

FEET—Ask the students the following questions, allowing time for answers after each.

- Where should the bear's feet be when the teacher is talking?
- What happens to the bear's whole body when the bear's feet start moving? (Student may wiggle the bear's feet to show what happens to its whole body.)

Put the stuffed bear away. Then continue the lesson by saying:

I want all of you to pretend to be poor listeners. Show me what the class would look like if every one of you were poor listeners. (As the students demonstrate poor listening, state aloud what you see.) I see people looking out the window, rummaging in their desks, getting on the floor, playing with a pencil. (Continue describing what the students are doing so that they may hear and feel how poor listening looks.)

Now I want all of you to show me how good listening looks. (As the students demonstrate good listening, state aloud what you see.) I see students sitting up straight in their seats, eyes looking this way, noses pointed toward me, hands and feet quiet. (Continue pointing out the qualities and parts of the body used in good listening.)

Ask the students:

What would I mean if, during my teaching, I said, "Hands, eyes, feet, nose, brain?" (I would be reminding the class to remember the parts the body that need to be used to achieve good listening.)

CONCLUSION:

Conclude the lesson by asking the students the following questions:

- Now that you have learned how the bear can be a better listener, can you tell me how you and the bear are alike? (Students have the same good-listening body parts as the bear.)
- How does listening help you learn? (You hear what is being said. Accept any other appropriate answers.)
- Why is good listening important? (Good listening helps you learn.)
- How is good listening similar to good manners? (It is polite to listen when someone is speaking to you.)

 STUDY SKILLS FUN! © 2003 MAR★CO PRODUCTS, INC. 1-800-448-2197

ACTION LISTENING AND FOCUSING SKILL ACTIVITIES

GRADE LEVEL: K-6

OBJECTIVE:
To help students develop listening skills
through active practice

USING EARS TO LISTEN:

1. **LISTENING WALK** (indoors or outdoors)
   Take the students on a "listening walk." Then discuss the different sounds that were heard. Have the students describe the quietest sounds, the loudest sounds, their favorite sounds, and their least favorite sounds. Ask the students to tell why the sounds were pleasant or unpleasant.

2. **FIND THE BELL**
   This activity requires a small bell. Ask one student to leave the group. That student will be the guessing student. Give a remaining group member a small bell to conceal and ring after the guessing student returns to the group. Tell the bell ringer to ring the bell only when the guessing student is looking in another direction. This insures that only the ears are used in this listening practice. After the guessing student has identified the student who is ringing the bell, conclude the activity by asking the guessing student questions that will tell what helped him/her identify the correct student. An example of a question could be, "Was it something you heard, saw, felt, or thought about that helped you identify the correct student?"

3. **BABY SOUNDS**
   Choose one student in the group to be a mother/father cat, chicken/rooster, pig, or other kind of animal. Then ask that student to leave the group. Choose another student from the group to make the animal sound the mother/father's baby would make. For example, a baby chick would say, "Peep, peep" if the mother/father were a chicken/rooster. Then assign a variety of other baby animal sounds to the other children in the group and ask them to QUIETLY make their sounds as the returning mother/father listens to determine which student is his/her baby. Ask the mother/father student to return to the group. Explain that one of the students in the group is his/her baby and can be found only by listening for its sound. Have the students begin making their sounds. Continue the game for as long as time allows, choosing a different animal for the mother/father each round.

4. **GUESS THE SOUND**
   Gather several different noise-making objects. For example, tap a pencil, blow a whistle, crumple paper, slap a ruler on a desk, and ring a bell. Also include such noises as clapping hands, stamping feet, clicking fingers, etc. Divide the students into two

teams. Have the students turn and face the back of the room. Explain that you will be making different noises and that a student who can identify the noise should raise his/her hand without turning around to face you. Explain that the person correctly identifying the noise will earn a point for his/her team. Begin the activity, choosing students from each team to identify alternate sounds.

Variation: Use pre-recorded animal sounds purchased on tape or CD or tape record various sounds to use in the game.

5. **STOP THE MUSIC**
    This activity requires a CD and CD player. Play fast-paced music and ask the students to dance in one spot or move in rhythm to the music. Tell the students to freeze or stop whenever the leader stops the music. Explain that a student caught moving will be a spotter for the next round, identifying anyone who moves after the music stops. When the spotter catches a person moving after the music stops, the newly caught student becomes the spotter and the previous spotter returns to the game.

6. **ACTION LISTENING**
    Divide the students into two teams. Ask one player from each team to come to the front of the room. Tell the players to listen carefully as you give several directions (hop on one foot, turn around twice, pat the top of your head, etc.), but not to perform any of the actions until you give them the signal to begin. Then say, "Go." Give points to the team whose player is the first to complete all of the actions.

    Depending on the age of the students, you may want to give one, two, or more directions at one time. If you are giving several directions, you may have to repeat them before the players begin. If you really want to get complicated, ask the students to perform only the third command.

7. **HUM DINGER**
    Ask three to five students to leave the room. Assign a different song to each person who leaves the room and tell the chosen students that when they return, each of them must find the students in the room who are humming "their" song. Assign the same songs in random order to the students left in the room. Tell the students to quietly hum their songs as the other players return to the room. Use simple songs such as *Row, Row, Row, Your Boat; Twinkle, Twinkle, Little Star; Mary Had A Little Lamb;* etc.

8. **MAIL BAG**
    Choose a leader. Ask the leader to call out descriptive statements like, "I have mail for everyone who is wearing tennis shoes, is wearing red, has long hair, is wearing a belt, is wearing stripes, etc." Explain that when the category called is relevant to anyone in the room, that person should quietly go to the front of the room. For example, if the caller says, "I have mail for girls with long hair," all girls with long hair should line up at the front of the room. Choose several students to be judges. The judges will determine whether some students did not line up when a category pertained to them. If someone caught standing should be sitting or is sitting when he/she should be standing, that person is removed from the game and serves as a judge until someone else is caught.

9. **CLAP OUT**

Choose a leader. Ask him/her to name four items. Three of the items should belong in the same category and one should not belong in that category. The leader then repeats the four items, challenging the students to clap when they hear the name of the item that does not belong in the same category as the other items. For example, banana, apple, hamburger (clap), pear. Students would clap when hearing the word *hamburger*, because it is a meat and does not belong with fruits. The students may be told the name of the category before the activity begins. Remind the students that the first time the four items are named, they are only to listen. The second time the items are named, they may clap at the appropriate time. Example of categories are meat; candy; things in the sky; water; trees; words with the same beginning sounds, ending sounds, vowel sounds; clothing; furniture; or games. The teacher may need to act as the leader until the students are able to perform the activity on their own.

10. **STORY CATCH**

For this activity, the leader will need to have a beanbag or small sponge ball. Tell the students that they will be telling a group story and how much time they have to complete the story. The leader will begin the story, then toss the beanbag or small sponge ball to another player. The player catching the beanbag or ball is to continue the story the first person began. The new storyteller must add at least three words before tossing the beanbag or ball to another player. The procedure continues until the allotted time has elapsed.

11. **PETE AND REPEAT**

Ask the students to sit in a circle. Choose a leader. Instruct the leader to state a message out loud to the player on his/her left. Tell the second person to pass the message out loud to the next person. Continue the activity until the message has traveled around the circle. The length of the message should reflect the group members' ability to repeat it.

12. **ACT OUT**

Ask the students to make up a story that has one main character. This character should be doing things that can be acted out by other students in the group. For example, "Once upon a time, there was a boy who woke up, stretched, yawned, rubbed his eyes, and jumped out of bed. He went to brush his teeth … etc." Choose one student to tell his/her story and three or more students to act out the story as they listen to the actions. Set a time limit for each story. Many students may just want to follow the pattern of a story that has been presented by another student and retell it with minor changes.

13. **STEAL THE BONE**

Choose a student to be the dog, and ask him/her to sit in a chair facing away from the group. Place an object (bone) on the floor behind the chair. Explain that the object of the game is to get the bone without the dog knowing it's being taken. In order to do this, anyone sneaking up behind the dog must be very quiet as the dog will be listening very carefully for any noise. If the dog hears a noise, the dog will bark and the person who was trying to take the bone must sit down. Choose a person to sneak up behind the dog. Continue choosing students to try to take the bone until one is successful. Allow the successful person to be the new dog.

14. **NAME THAT SOUND/TUNE/PERSON**
Choose a student to make a sound and ask others to identify it. Sounds may include animal noises, transportation, musical instruments, etc. A variation would be for each player to hum or whistle a simple tune while the other students attempt to name it. Another variation is to blindfold a player and ask another player to stand in front of the blindfolded person and make a noise (animal noise, truck, speaking). The object is for the blindfolded person to name the person making the noise.

15. **FIND THE DOE DOE BIRD**
Choose two students to leave the room. Choose another student in the room to be the Doe Doe Bird. Ask everyone else in the group to sing *Row, Row, Row Your Boat* while the Doe Doe Bird sings "Doe doe, doe, doe, doe" over and over to the same tune as the group song. When the students return to the room, they will try to be the first player to find the Doe Doe Bird within a certain amount of time.

16. **CONNECT**
This activity requires a soft sponge ball or beanbag. The leader should tell the students that he/she will throw the sponge ball/beanbag to one student and at the same time say a sentence that is correct, "birds fly," or incorrect, "horses fly." If the statement is correct the player catching the ball must repeat the sentence, then say either the same sentence or a new sentence and throw the ball to another player. If the sentence is incorrect, the player catching the ball must correct the sentence and throw the ball to a new player. Players may purposely give a wrong answer to try to trick the person who is catching the ball/beanbag. Other ideas for statements are "boats float," trees burn," and "elephants walk."

17. **HOT NUMBER**
For this activity, the leader needs a watch with a second hand. Randomly assign each student a number between one and the number of students in the group. Explain that the students are to keep their numbers secret. Tell the first player that he/she has five seconds to call out any number except his/her own. The player whose number is called then has five seconds to call out another number. A player who fails to call out a number within five seconds is removed from the game until the next person makes a mistake. The person who has been removed from the game may serve as a monitor for spotting the next mistake. The object of this game is for students to be able to quickly call out another number, quickly respond when their own number is called, and respond only when their number is called.

Variation: Ask the person calling out the number to spin a Frisbee® or strong paper plate on the floor while calling out the number. The person assigned that number must catch the spinning object before it stops spinning and falls down. Then that person spins the object again and calls out another number.

18. **REFLECTION**

Divide the students into pairs and have them face their partners. One partner is selected to be the pointer. The leader then quickly calls out appropriate body parts, and the pointer points to those parts on his/her partner's body. After a few calls have been made, have the partners change positions. Be sure to emphasize that no touching is allowed and that anyone who does touch his/her partner, will be removed from the game.

19. **FAIRY TALE TIME**

Ask one student to tell the story of a well-known favorite fairy tale while other students perform the actions of the character or characters. Encourage the characters to add extemporaneous dialogue as the storyteller pauses. Simple props or costumes can add to the excitement. The number of characters needed depends upon the fairy tale. For example, *The Three Bears* will have four characters: Goldilocks, Papa Bear, Mama Bear, and Baby Bear.

20. **SILLY PUTTY**

Reproduce the *Silly Putty® Directions* (included on CD). Divide the students into pairs. Tell each pair of students to choose one partner to follow the directions and the other partner to assist him/her in keeping his/her balance as he/she follows the directions. Then, using the *Silly Putty Directions*, call out the directions to the pairs. (**Note**: If necessary, instruct the students not to touch one another in any inappropriate body part during this activity.)

21. **GROUP JUGGLE**

This activity requires a soft sponge ball or beanbag. Have the students form a circle. Begin by calling out a student's name and tossing the ball/beanbag to him/her. That player then calls out another student's name and throws the ball/beanbag to that player. Time the juggle and encourage the players to throw the ball/beanbag faster.

22. **NAME THE OBJECT**

Print and cut apart three copies of the the *Name The Object Drawing Cards* (included on CD). Divide the class into three groups—A, B, and C. Then divide the students in each group into pairs and have each pair of students decide which partner will hold the card. Distribute one *Name The Object Drawing Card* to that person, emphasizing that the other partner should not see it. The partner with the card then reads the directions. The listening partner draws in the air or in his/her mind what is being described, then tries to guess what the object is. When the listening partner has guessed correctly or the allotted time has elapsed, have the partner holding the *Name The Object Drawing Card* give the card to another listening partner in the same group. For example, a partner in the A group who correctly described the drawing card will give his/her card to another partner who was a listener in the A group in the previous round. That person then becomes the partner who describes and his/her partner becomes the listener. Continue the game for six rounds, until each group has used each card.

23. **BUILD IT & THEY WILL COME**

This activity requires Playdough®, toothpicks and the *Build It & They Will Come Cards* (included on CD). Reproduce enough cards for each group of three students to have one at a time. Divide the students into groups of three. Distribute a small bag of 32 or more toothpicks, a ball of Playdough and a card depicting a simple design using toothpicks and small balls of Playdough. Select one player to look at the design card and describe to the others how the toothpicks and Playdough balls are positioned. The other players listen to the full description (or follow each direction as it is given), then use the toothpicks and Playdough to make the design they think is on the card. After the students have completed their designs, they look at the card to see how carefully they listened to the description. Have two of the players switch roles. The person describing the design should come to the leader and be given another design card. Play one more time, giving everyone in the group an opportunity to be both a leader and a listener.

24. **DON'T BOTHER ME**

Divide the students into groups of two. Have one partner be the speaker and the other the listener. The speaker will then begin to talk about a good trip, favorite teacher, favorite movie, favorite story, or something else of interest. The listener responds by using poor listening skills, such as looking away from the speaker, trying to talk about something else, wiggling, etc. When the allotted time has elapsed, the partners should switch roles. When each student has been both listener and speaker, the partners can discuss what happened during the poor-listening time.

Variation: First practice poor listening skills, then do good listening skills, noting the difference good listening skills made for each player.

25. **NAME THAT WORD**

Print and cut apart a set of *Name That Word Cards* (included on CD) for each student group. Rubber band a set of cards together for each student group. Divide the students into small groups and give each group a set of cards, paper, and a pencil. When the leader says, "Go," one member of each small group takes a card and begins to draw on a sheet of paper a picture of the word. The student in the group who guesses what word is being depicted gets the card to hold and earns a point. A new person then gets to take a card and draw for the other students in his/her group. The person with the most cards in each group wins.

26. **DUNK IT**

This activity requires a large paper bag and four sheets of crumpled paper for each group. Divide the students into small groups of five or six members. Distribute a large paper bag and four sheets of crumpled paper to each group. Designate one group member as a helper. The helper stands next to the paper bag placed on the floor while the others line up one to two feet from the bag with their backs toward it. The helper tells the thrower of the paper balls the directions for throwing the ball into the bag and dunking it. Players get one point for each dunk. Players take turns being the helper.

27. CONNECT THE DOTS

For this activity, you will need *Dot-To-Dot Pictures* (several have been included on the CD or you may use your own) for each student and a pencil and blindfold for each pair of students. Divide the students into pairs. Blindfold one member of the pair and give that person a pencil. The dot-to-dot picture is placed in front of the blindfolded player. The other partner tells the blindfolded player where to place the pencil on the picture and how to move it. When the picture is completed or time is called, switch roles, giving the newly blindfolded student a new dot-to-dot picture. When each student has had a chance to be blindfolded and to be the blindfolded player's partner, see who listened well enough to complete the dot-to-dot picture. (***Note:*** If using a blindfold is inappropriate, have the students tightly close their eyes.)

ACTION LISTENING AND FOCUSING SKILL ACTIVITIES

GRADE LEVEL: K-6

OBJECTIVE:

To help students develop listening skills through active practice using their eyes and ears

USING EYES AND EARS TO LISTEN:

1. **PATTERN LISTENING**
    For this activity, the leader may need a ball. Clap out a pattern or bounce a ball in a pattern. For example, clap twice, pause, clap once. Ask the students to repeat the pattern. The listeners may begin by watching and listening. Then after memorizing the pattern, the students try to duplicate the pattern with their backs facing the leader.

2. **PHONE MESSAGES**
    This activity requires two play phones or two real cell phones that have been turned off. Select a student to perform the activity with the leader. Have both participants use a phone. The leader pretends to call the student volunteer and leave a message, including a phone number so the call can be returned, for that person's mother or father. Begin by using a phone number with three digits. Progress to more digits when the students are ready for the difficulty to be increased. If necessary, the players may dial the numbers to visually enhance listening skills and memory. To verify that the student has correctly heard the message, have him/her repeat the message aloud or write it on a note pad.

3. **NAME GAME**
    Ask four to six students to come to the front of the group and state their names. Then ask one student in the class to recall the names in the order in which they were given. This is an excellent activity to use at the beginning of the year when the students are not yet familiar with everyone in the room.

4. **POEM "WILLIE MCGURGLE"**
    Reproduce *Willie McGurgle* (included on CD). This activity can be presented in two ways—as a listening art activity or as a listening role-play activity. If it is being used as an art activity, the materials needed are drawing paper and crayons or colored markers. If it is being used as a role-play activity, the materials needed are colored paper, masking tape, costumes, and props.

    Listening Art Activity—Distribute art paper and crayons or colored markers to each student. Read the *Willie McGurgle* poem (included on CD) aloud, encouraging the students to visualize what they hear. When you have finished reading the poem,

 STUDY SKILLS FUN! © 2003 MAR★CO PRODUCTS, INC. 1-800-448-2197

have the students draw and color Willie McGurgle. Tell the students to include in their drawings as many details as they can remember. Compare the drawings to see who remembered the most details.

Listening Role-Play Activity—To present the role-play activity, you will need a black umbrella, brown sweater or jacket, old shoes, and pieces of colored paper that match the colors mentioned in the poem. Read the poem aloud, encouraging the students to visualize what they hear. Select a volunteer to come to the front of the room. Ask the students to name the clothes that Willie was wearing and have the volunteer put on the shoes and jacket or sweater as they are mentioned. This will create visual stimulation and motivate memory. Then have the students name the colors and body parts mentioned in the poem. As the students are doing this, tape a matching patch of colored paper on or near the appropriate body part on the volunteer. Conclude the exercise by having the students describe what Willie took when he left town, and have the volunteer pick up the umbrella and walk out of the room.

> Did you ever hear of Willie McGurgle
> Who limped around town with his nose painted purple?
> He was the ugliest man I ever have seen,
> One eye was orange, the other was green.
> Yellow hair hung down like straw on his head,
> He dressed all in brown with patches of red,
> Out of beat-up old shoes his poor toes stuck through,
> In very cold weather, his toes turned blue.
> One day in the rain beneath an umbrella of black,
> Willie left town, and he never came back.
>
> -Author Unknown

5. **BALL TOSS**
   This activity requires a small sponge ball or beanbag. Have the students form a circle. Give one player the ball/beanbag and have him/her name a favorite thing (favorite color, ice cream, subject, sport, etc.). Then the player will toss the sponge ball/beanbag to another player. The player catching the ball must tell what the previous person said and then, using the same topic, state his/her own answer. Change the topic after about five tosses.

6. **BIG BIRD SAYS**
   Tell the students they are to follow the leader's directions only if the leader says, "Big Bird says." Explain that the leader might visually give different directions from the directions he/she gives aloud. For example, the leader may leave his/her hands down while saying, "Big Bird says to raise your hands." Someone caught not doing what Big Bird says may serve as a spotter to identify the next person who doesn't do as Big Bird says. The identified person then becomes the spotter and the previous spotter rejoins the group.

7. **MATCH A FRIEND**

Divide the students into two groups. Ask the first group to respond orally to a question the leader asks. Tell the second group to listen to the question and to the answer to see if their answer would be the same as that of someone in the first group. For example, the leader could ask, "How many brothers do you have?" The students in the first group would answer the question. Then ask the students in the second group to take turns responding to the same question by stating the name of the player in the first group who gave the same response. For example: John, a student in the first group, said he has two brothers. A student in the second group who also has two brothers would answer, "John matches me because he has two brothers and I do, too."

The game may be played a number of ways. Each student can answer the same question or the leader may choose to ask different questions each time. Methods of playing will depend on the age and level of development of the group. Possible subjects for questions are: number of sisters/brothers, type of pets, favorite song, favorite school subject, birthday month, hobbies, trips, favorite color, and favorite sport.

8. **SHARE SOMETHING**

Ask the students to form pairs. Select a subject, then tell each person in the pair to tell something about him/ herself that relates to the subject. For example, something funny he/she did as a baby, an accident he/she has had, something scary he/she remembers, his/her best birthday. Instruct each pair to join another pair. Each student should introduce his/her partner to the other pair and share what the partner has said on the subject chosen. Ask these two pairs to join another group of four, making eight, and continue in the same manner to share what the original partner said or what one of the other persons in the group of four had said.

9. **WHAT SWIMS?**

Tell the students that they will be hearing some words that name things that swim or are able to stay in the water (fish, porpoise, boat, people, etc.). They will also be hearing other words. Explain that if the word called names something that can swim or stay in the water, the students are to make swimming motions with their arms. If the word called names something that cannot swim or stay in the water, such as a shoe or table, they are to put their arms by their sides. A student who makes a mistake will serve as a spotter watching for the next player who makes a mistake in listening. When a spotter identifies a student making a mistake, the students change places and the student who made the mistake becomes the spotter. The original spotter returns to the group. Adaptations of this activity would be to call out: things that fly (arm flapping motion), things that go in the mouth (feeding motion), things that move (wiggling action), people you trust (hugging motion), things that walk (marching in place).

 STUDY SKILLS FUN! © 2003 MAR*CO PRODUCTS, INC. 1-800-448-2197

10. **THE WAVE**

Ask the students to stand in a straight line. The student at the head of the line is the leader. Instruct the first student in line to perform a movement, such as raising his/her left arm. The other students in the line take turns imitating the same movement, beginning with the person directly behind the leader and continuing to the end of the line. The leader then goes to the end of the line and the second person in line becomes the leader, continuing the game.

11. **HAND SIGNS**

Have the students practice matching hand signs with sounds. For example, making a fist (a growling sound), holding up five fingers (a moo), a raised hand (a sneeze), a tap on the head (a meow). Add other signs according to the age of the group. Divide the students into three or four small groups. Assign each group, or person, if there are a small number of students, a specific hand sign and sound or movement. The leader then begins making hand signs. When the hand signs are given, the group or person having the corresponding sound or movement must respond with that sound or movement within five seconds. For the first round, show the signs in the order in which they were assigned. Then change the sequence of the hand signs. As the game progresses, add signs for loudness and softness or perform two or more signs at the same time.

12. **RAINSTORM**

Have the students sit in a circle. Tell the students they are going to make a rainstorm. Explain that they will do this by performing a series of actions to make sounds. The leader will begin the activity by performing an action. One after the other, each member of the circle will then perform the same action. As the sound continues around the circle in a wave effect, the leader begins another sound. It is important that each person continues to make the first sound before adding an additional sound. The first action sound to make a rainstorm is to rub your palms together and make a swishing noise (wind). Then click your fingers (rain), hit your hands on your thighs (harder rain), and stomp your feet (thunder). Reverse the sequence as the storm dissipates.

ACTION LISTENING AND FOCUSING SKILL ACTIVITIES

GRADE LEVEL: K-6

OBJECTIVE:
To help students develop listening skills
by using messages from
body language, eyes, and ears

USING BODY LANGUAGE TO LISTEN:

1. **WHAT AM I DRAWING?**
    This activity requires art paper and a pencil for each student. Distribute art paper and a pencil to each student. Explain that each of the students will be making a secret drawing that will require them to listen and follow directions very carefully.

    A variation of the activity involves dividing the group into pairs. Have one partner turn his/her back toward the other partner. The partner facing the other partner's back listens to the drawing directions from the leader and draws, with one finger, on his/her partner's back. That partner tries to guess what the drawing is. Use simple drawings and simple directions such as the following:

    *   Draw an large upside-down ∩.
    *   Draw a small upside-down ∩ on top of the large ∩.
    *   Draw a straight line halfway down the center of the large ∩, then draw a crooked line at the bottom of the straight line.
    *   Draw a half-circle (on each side) from the top of the small ∩, extending the half-circle halfway down the side of the large ∩.

    (This drawing should look like the back of an elephant.)

2. **TWINS**
    Have the students sit in a circle. Ask a student to make a distorted face and look at the person on his/her right. Tell this person to try to make the same face back at the person who made the face to him/her. Then ask the second player to turn to his/her right and make a different face which the person on his/her right tries to imitate. Proceed around the circle, with each student making a new distorted face that the person on his/her right tries to imitate.

3. **MIRROR IMAGE**
    Divide the students into pairs and have them face one other. Tell the students to imitate each other's movements in such a way that someone watching could not tell which student is the leader and which is the follower.

4. **SILENCE IS GOLDEN**

Explain to the students that the leader will pose in different facial and body positions. Some of the poses will be friendly. Others will be unfriendly. The students are to stand up if the leader's pose is friendly and sit down if it is unfriendly. Remind the students that if they encounter a teacher in an unfriendly pose outside of this activity they must decide whether they should correct their behavior or change what they are doing in order to comply with the rules. If the unfriendly pose is assumed by someone the student wants as a friend, the student should consider choosing someone else with whom to play. If the unfriendly pose is assumed by a parent, the student should consider staying away from the parent for a while or try to correct the situation that could have caused the parent's reaction.

GESTURE	MEANING
smile	friendly
nodding head "Yes"	friendly
shaking head "No"	unfriendly
winking an eye	friendly
shrugging shoulders	unfriendly
frown	unfriendly
hand on heart	friendly
tapping foot	unfriendly
drumming fingers	unfriendly
doodling while listening	unfriendly
hugging	friendly
standing tall, making good eye contact	friendly
eyes narrowed	unfriendly
shaking fist	unfriendly
lowering head, looking at floor	unfriendly
roll eyes, look disgusted	unfriendly

(**Note:** Some unfriendly gestures may result from sadness, loneliness, or boredom.)

5. **CREATION**

Reproduce and cut apart a set of *Creation Word Cards* (included on CD) for each group of students. Divide the students into small groups and give each group a set of cards and clay. Have the students place the *Creation Word Cards* face down in the middle of the group. Tell the students to take turns drawing a card, which no one but them is allowed to see. The person drawing the card should then use the clay to shape the object for the word written on the card, until someone in the group guesses what the object is. Each correct answer earns a point for the team member.

ACTION LISTENING AND FOCUSING SKILL ACTIVITIES
GRADE LEVEL: K-6

OBJECTIVE:
To help students develop listening skills by using messages from their mind, eyes, and ears and interpreting the body language of others

USING MIND, EYES, EARS, AND BODY LANGUAGE TO LISTEN:

1. **GET-TOGETHER GAME**
   Divide the class into small groups and have each group select a leader. The leaders should then ask each of their group members one of the questions using the *Get-Together Game Cards* (included on CD). After hearing the answers, the group leaders should report from memory their group's information to the other groups. The students who listened to the report are then given an opportunity to recall what was said and earn a point for their group for each correct answer. A new leader can be chosen for each round.

2. **HAPPY TRAVELER**
   This activity can be used with the whole class or a smaller number of students. If you are using this activity with the whole class, read the *Happy Traveler* story (included on CD) aloud and have the students act out the actions as they are mentioned. If you are using this activity with a smaller number of students, follow the same procedure having one student at a time act out the actions. Repeat the activity until all the students in the group have been included.

   > The Happy Traveler got out of bed, brushed his teeth, put on his clothes, and went downstairs. He ate his cereal, then opened the door, and went for a walk. He walked and walked and walked and walked. He looked to the north, then to the south, then to the east, and finally to the west. He climbed a tree and looked all around. He climbed down the tree and sat down on a big rock. The rock started moving back and forth. Finally it stood up and let out a huge growl. The rock was a bear! The Happy Traveler ran back home, opened the door, closed the door, and locked it. He sat down in a big chair, wiped his forehead, and panted. Was he ever glad to be back home, safe, and sound!

3. **CAN YOU DO IT?**
   Whisper one direction to a player and instruct him/her to follow that direction. If necessary, repeat the directions one time. Points may be given if the directions are

completed correctly. As the players' skills improve, increase the difficulty by giving more than one direction at a time. Some suggested directions are:

Name your favorite holiday.
Shake hands with another person in the group.
Run in place.
Name your favorite car.
Pretend to spin a hula hoop.
Turn around in a circle.
Act like your favorite animal.
Say something nice to someone in the group.
Name your favorite flavor of ice cream.
Introduce one person in the group to another person in the group.
Do 12 jumping jacks.

4. **GOING ON VACATION**

Ask the first person in the group to begin by saying, "I'm going on vacation and I'm going to take …" Ask the next person to repeat what the first person said and add a new item. Continue the game by having each player repeat what the person before him/her said and adding one new item. The object of the game is to see how many items can be added without forgetting previously stated items. Use items beginning with a single letter of the alphabet, such as all A's, or name things in alphabetical order.

5. **TELL ABOUT IT**

Divide the group into two teams. Tell the students that they will be given a topic to talk about and that you will award points to the team of any student who can repeat what a player from the other team has said. Give one team a topic and give the team members time to respond. Then ask the members of the other team to remember as much about the discussed topic they can. Repeat the procedure, assigning a topic to the other team. You may award points for the number of correct responses. Possible topics include:

What did you do during summer vacation?
What do you want to be when you grow up and why?
What is the most exciting thing you have ever done?
What is the most frightening thing you have ever done?

6. **TREASURE HUNT**

Reproduce and cut apart the *Treasure Hunt Cards* (included on CD). Place the cards face-down in front of the group. Choose one person to be the *treasure hunter* and ask him/her to take a question card from the stack and read the question aloud. Tell the players to stand if they can respond positively to the question on the card. Ask the *treasure hunter* to quickly take note of all who are standing, then tell the students who are standing to sit down. The *treasure hunter* then tries to recall the names of the players who were standing. You may award points if the student can name everyone who stood up.

7. **TRAIN**

Choose one player to be the engineer. Ask the engineer to go to another player, stand in front of that person with his/her back toward the other player, and ask, "What is your name?" Instruct this player to state his/her name while placing his/her hands on the engineer's shoulders. Then have these two players travel to another player and ask for the name of that person. At this point, the engineer (front person) must say the names of all of the people behind him/her. If the engineer cannot do this correctly, the next person in line becomes the engineer and the previous engineer goes to the end of the train. After the engineer names everyone aboard the train four or five times, he/she moves to the end of the line. The student who is now at the head of the line becomes the engineer.

8. **MY NAME IS …**

Have the students sit in a circle. Select one person to begin the activity by stating his/her name and an adjective that describes himself/herself that begins with the same first letter as his/her name. For example, the player may say, "My name is Magnificent Mary" or "My name is Caring Candace." Tell the next person to state the name and adjective previously stated, then add his/her name with an adjective. Continue the procedure around the circle, having each player state the names and adjectives previous stated and adding his/her name and adjective to the list. See how many names and adjectives the players can remember. When everyone has participated, have the first person in the circle tell the names and adjectives of everyone in the circle.

9. **IF YOU WERE …**

Call three to six players to the front of the room. Ask them a category question such as, "If you were a zoo animal, what would you be and why?" (You may use farm animals, forest animals, cartoon characters, superheroes, etc.) After all of these students have answered, ask the remaining students to state the name of each student and his/her answer to the question.

10. **FIND A PERSON WHO**

Decide on a topic and announce it to the class. Have five to seven student volunteers come to the front of the room and talk about the chosen topic. When the students are finished, repeat the process with different topics and different students. After completing several rounds, challenge the class to name the students and what they said about the topics.

Some suggested topics are:

> A book read in the past two weeks
> A musical talent
> A recent camping trip
> Going horseback riding
> A newly learned skill
> Meeting a celebrity

 STUDY SKILLS FUN! © 2003 MAR∗CO PRODUCTS, INC. 1-800-448-2197

Visiting another country
Taking gymnastics
Taking karate
Taking dancing lessons
Having a scary dream
Going skiing

11. MAGIC DISAPPEARANCE

This activity requires collecting several objects and bringing them to the session along with a large cloth. Place several objects on a table in front of the group. Tell the students to look carefully at the objects. Allow the students to look at the objects for about one minute, then cover the objects with the cloth. Challenge the students to determine who can remember the most objects. The players may either list the objects on paper or simply state the names of the objects when you call on them.

12. INTERVIEW REVIEW

Have the students form pairs. Tell the students that each of them is going to conduct an interview with his/her partner. Explain that, through the interview, each student should attempt to find out as much as possible about his/her partner. Some topics for interview questions are: number of family members, favorite activities, best school subjects, etc. Tell the students to decide who will begin the interview and tell them how much time they will have to complete the interview. When the allotted time has elapsed, have the partners switch positions and repeat the procedure. After each partner has been interviewed, each set of partners should join with another pair. Then each person in the new group should be introduced by name along with the information obtained in the interview. Each group of four may then pair up with another group of four and continue the introductions.

13. PASS IT ON

This activity requires that several objects be placed in a paper bag. Have the students sit in a circle. Select one person to take one object such as a key, pencil, or book from the bag. That person should tell what the item is, say something about it, and pass it to the next person. The person receiving the object immediately repeats what was said by the previous player and adds information about the object that will begin a story. As the object is passed around the circle, each player receiving it immediately repeats what was said previously and adds to the story. The last player receiving the object completes the story with an appropriate ending.

14. VIP

Ask one person to pretend to be a famous person who is alive or dead. The other students then ask questions of the *famous person* in order to determine his/her identity. They may ask only questions that can be answered with either "yes" or "no." A variation would be for the player to pretend to be an object with the other players asking questions to find out the name of the object.

15. **DON'T GIVE ME THAT!**
This activity requires access to a second hand on a clock, watch, or stopwatch. Divide the group into two teams. Explain that each team will be asked questions and, if answered correctly, earn points. The questions can be answered with words such as perhaps, maybe, affirmative, negative, etc., but may not be answered with the words "yes" or "no." If the correct answer is given in less than five seconds or within a time appropriate for the age of the players, the player may come to the front of the room. If they answer slowly or incorrectly or by using "yes" or "no," they must stay in their seats. The team with the most students at the front of the room at the end of the round is the winner. The leader may use questions such as:

Is it spring?
Can you dance?
Do you know how to sing *Twinkle, Twinkle, Little Star*?

16. **BUZZ**
Ask the players to choose a number between two and nine. Instruct the group to take turns counting out loud, beginning with the number one and moving in sequence. Whenever the count reaches the selected number or a multiple of that number, tell the players to say, "Buzz" instead of the predetermined number. For example: if the selected number was two: 1, 2 **Buzz**, 3, 4 **Buzz**, 5, 6 **Buzz**, 7, 8 **Buzz**, 9, 10 **Buzz**. If a mistake is made, the group must begin counting again. This activity is an excellent practice for math skills.

LISTENING ACTION STORIES

GRADE LEVEL: K-5 (Older students may need some adaptations)

PURPOSE: To practice good listening by hearing and responding as needed

OBJECTIVE: To respond orally or physically to information heard

MATERIALS: ☐ Copy of a *Listening Action Story* (Included on CD)

PRE-LESSON PREPARATION: These activities may be performed with the whole group responding with the designated sounds, actions, or words. You may also decide to divide the large group into three or more smaller groups, depending upon the age of the students. If you are using smaller groups, each small group is responsible only for specifically assigned sounds, actions, or words.

PROCEDURE:

Before reading each *Listening Action Story*, tell the students:

I will be reading a story to you. Please listen carefully for certain cues that will let you know when to make specific sounds, perform actions, or say certain words that will help in telling and enjoying the story. I will also be emphasizing, with my voice, when a cue is given in the story. At times, I may speed up the reading of the story to make recognizing and responding to cues even more challenging.

TWISTED LISTENING
LISTENING ACTION GUIDANCE ACTIVITY

GRADE LEVEL: K-5

PURPOSE: To be able to recognize good and poor listening skills

OBJECTIVE: To earn points by modeling the correct body reaction to good and poor listening skills

MATERIALS:
☐ *Twisted Listening* (included on CD)
☐ *Silly Putty® Directions* (included on CD)

PRE-LESSON PREPARATION: Print *Twisted Listening*. Make a list of twisted body positions or use the positions listed on the *Silly Putty® Directions*.

PROCEDURE:

Tell the students:

I will call out a twisted body position such as right elbow to your right knee. Then I will call out a listening skill. It may be a good skill or a poor one. If it is a good listening skill, just stand straight with your hands at your sides. If it is a poor listening skill, quickly perform the twisted body motion that was named. If I see an incorrect body motion, that person sits down until the next person makes a mistake. At that time, the first person rejoins the game and the last person to make a mistake sits out until another person makes a mistake. (**Note:** If appropriate for your students' grade level, choose leaders from those students who consistently perform the correct motions to continue the game.)

Optional alternative: After students have learned the game, divide them into small groups with leaders.

Begin the activity by reading aloud the first body position and a study skill from *Twisted Listening*.

FOLLOW-UP:

At the conclusion of the activity, ask the students the following questions:

▸ What helped you recognize good and poor listening skills?
▸ Which good listening skills do you see your friends using in class?

STUDY SKILLS FUN! © 2003 MAR✶CO PRODUCTS, INC. 1-800-448-2197

PICTURE THIS
LISTENING ACTION GUIDANCE ACTIVITY

GRADE LEVEL:	2-5
PURPOSE:	To practice taking in needed information by listening with your eyes
OBJECTIVE:	To become champion listeners by correctly answering questions about pictures
MATERIALS:	☐ Several pictures, such as from calendars (More detailed pictures should be used with older students.)
PRE-LESSON PREPARATION:	Collect a variety of pictures on different themes and mount them on heavy paper. Prepare who, what, where, when, how, and why questions for each picture to be used.

PROCEDURE:

Tell the students:

I will divide the students into pairs and show the whole class a picture to study. The picture will then be placed out of sight, and I will call four sets of partners to the front of the class to answer questions about the picture. The partners may help one other remember the details of the picture.

Each set of partners will take turns answering who, what, where, when, how, and why questions about the picture. If the answer is correct, the partners will stay at the front of the room. If the answer is incorrect, another set of partners will replace them. After all the questions have been answered correctly, the sets of partners remaining at the front of the room will be declared Champion Eye Listeners. We will recognize them with applause before they sit down.

When all the questions about a picture have been answered, select another group of partners and repeat the procedure with a new picture.

FOLLOW-UP:

At the conclusion of the activity, ask the students the following questions:

▸ What helped you remember details about the pictures?
▸ How can you picture things in your mind?

PAY ATTENTION
LISTENING ACTION GUIDANCE ACTIVITY

GRADE LEVEL: 3-5

PURPOSE: To practice listening with your ears, eyes, body language, and mind

OBJECTIVE: To earn the most play money for your team by correctly answering the *Pay Attention Cards*

MATERIALS:
- [ ] *Pay Attention Cards* (included on CD)
- [ ] $100 bills and $500 bills (included on CD)
- [ ] 5 different colors of 9″x 12″ construction paper:
     - 8 pieces of blue (ears)
     - 8 pieces of red (body)
     - 8 pieces of yellow (eyes)
     - 8 pieces of green (mind)
     - 4 pieces of black (start & finish)
  or 36 paper plates and markers
- [ ] Die

PRE-LESSON PREPARATION: Divide the construction paper into two equal sets. (Each set should include: four blue rectangles, four red rectangles, four yellow rectangles, four green rectangles, and two black rectangles.) You may also use white paper plates with the colors placed in the middle of the plates. Print the following on medium- or heavy-weight paper:

Pay Attention Mind Cards (green)
Pay Attention Body Language Cards (orange)
Pay Attention Eyes Cards (yellow)
Pay Attention Ears Cards (blue)
5 copies of the $100 bills (green)
1 copy of the $500 bills (green)

Cut apart the cards and bills. Optional: Laminate the colored rectangles, cards, and bills for durability.

 STUDY SKILLS FUN! © 2003 MAR∗CO PRODUCTS, INC. 1-800-448-2197

PROCEDURE:

With the construction paper rectangles, make two parallel "trails" in the front of the room. Have each trail begin and end with a black rectangle. Tell the students:

I will choose two teams. Each team will begin with five $100 bills. One person from each team will come to the front of the room and stand on the black rectangle at the beginning of the trail. That person will be the traveling team member for that turn only. The trails will go across the front of the room side by side. The next member of each team will throw the die for the traveling team member when it's that team's turn and will also read the *Pay Attention Card* that matches the color the traveling team member lands upon. Each color stands for something different and asks questions about something different. The blue cards stand for ears, the orange stand for body language, the yellow for eyes, and the green cards for the mind. The number on the die is the number of spaces that the traveling member moves on the trail. If the traveling team member answers the question correctly, the team earns a $100 bill. If the question is answered incorrectly, the team pays the other team a $100 bill. After the traveling member has answered the *Pay Attention Card*, his/her turn is over and the next person on the team takes his/her place on the same rectangle. The team earns another $100 bill for reaching the black rectangle at the end of the trail. Count the money won by each team. The team with the most money wins the round. Continue playing rounds until the allotted time has elapsed.

Select the teams, distribute the $100 bills, and begin the game. (**Note:** In order to have enough $100 bills to play the game, when a team earns five $100 bills they should exchange them for one $500 bill.)

FOLLOW-UP:

At the conclusion of the activity, ask the students the following questions:

▸ Which is the best way for you to listen: by feelings, pictures, body language, or remembering techniques?
▸ What is an example of one of the ways of listening?

MIXED-UP LISTENING
LISTENING ACTION GUIDANCE ACTIVITY

GRADE LEVEL: 1-5

PURPOSE: To recognize directions by listening and responding to the information given quickly and correctly

OBJECTIVE: To become *It* by responding quickly and correctly when your number is called

MATERIALS:
☐ Index cards
☐ Marker

PRE-LESSON PREPARATION: Number as many index cards as there are students who will be participating in the activity. Make two sets. (Only one set of cards is needed if you think the players will not easily forget their number. In this case, whisper a different number to each player and use only one set for calling out the numbers. Do not give the numbers in sequence.)

PROCEDURE:

Tell the students:

I will give each player a number to remember. (Older students may be assigned bigger numbers.) The numbers will be assigned in random order or mixed up. I will choose two people to be *It*. The *Its* will each draw a number from the stack of number cards and call it out. If one of the *Its* draws his or her own number, the card must be put back into the stack and a new card should be drawn. The players who have the called numbers must stand immediately, call out "(THEIR NUMBER) is listening," and change seats with each other. For example, if your number is two and that number is called out, you must immediately stand up to see with whom to exchange seats, and also call out, "Two is listening."

If the players whose numbers are called out do not call out that they are listening and change seats by the time the two *Its* count down from ten, then the two *Its* remain *It*. But if the players do call out and change seats before the countdown is completed, the two new players, whose numbers were called, then become *It*.

 STUDY SKILLS FUN! © 2003 MAR✶CO PRODUCTS, INC. 1-800-448-2197

Demonstrate the speed at which the *Its* should count from 10 to 1. If necessary, have the class practice counting until everyone is counting at the same speed. Then choose the first two *Its* and proceed with the game.

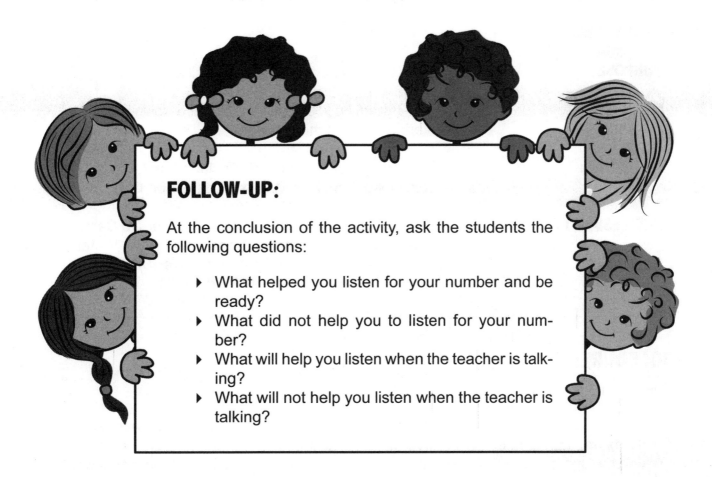

FOLLOW-UP:

At the conclusion of the activity, ask the students the following questions:

- ▸ What helped you listen for your number and be ready?
- ▸ What did not help you to listen for your number?
- ▸ What will help you listen when the teacher is talking?
- ▸ What will not help you listen when the teacher is talking?

LISTENING COVER-UP
LISTENING ACTION GUIDANCE ACTIVITY

GRADE LEVEL:	K-2
PURPOSE:	To practice listening and thinking skills
OBJECTIVE:	To win by turning your picture cards face-down, thereby covering up all of the pictures
MATERIALS:	☐ *Listening Cover-Up Cards* (included on CD) ☐ *Listening Cover-Up Words* (included on CD)
PRE-LESSON PREPARATION:	Print and cut apart enough *Listening Cover-Up Cards* so each student has three of each card (Fire, Water Ground, Sky). Print the *Listening Cover-Up Words*. Optional: Laminate the cards for durability.

PROCEDURE:

Tell the students:

I will give each of you three *Listening Cover-Up Cards*. The cards might have different pictures on them, or they might have matching pictures. The pictures are of the sky, the water, the ground, and fire. I will call out a word. If you have a picture that shows where that word would be found most of the time, you will turn that one card face-down, and "cover up" the picture. Turn only one card face-down, even if you have another card with the same picture. For example, if I say, "Bird," and you have a picture of the sky, you would turn over a picture of the sky, because birds can usually be found flying in the sky.

Remember, turn over only one *Listening Cover-Up Card* for each word called. Call out "Cover-up" when all three of your cards have been turned face-down. I will then check your cards. We might begin a new game after a winner is declared, or we might continue playing until the second- and third-place winners call out, "Cover-up."

Begin the game by reading words from the *Listening Cover-Up Words* list.

FOLLOW-UP:

At the conclusion of the activity, ask the students the following questions:

▸ What helped you listen for a name to go with your pictures?

▸ What would help you listen for the teacher's directions in class?

STUDY SKILLS FUN! © 2003 MAR*CO PRODUCTS, INC. 1-800-448-2197

PAY ATTENTION TO ME NOW
LISTENING ACTION GUIDANCE ACTIVITY

GRADE LEVEL: 3-6

PURPOSE: To practice listening with your ears, eyes, body language, and mind

OBJECTIVE: To win by collecting the most $100 bills in play money for your group

MATERIALS:
- ☐ *Pay Attention Cards* (included on CD)
- ☐ $100 bills and $500 bills (included on CD)
- ☐ Markers
- ☐ Die

PRE-LESSON PREPARATION: Print the following on medium- or heavy-weight paper:

Pay Attention Mind Cards (green)
Pay Attention Body Language Cards (orange)
Pay Attention Eyes Cards (yellow)
Pay Attention Ears Cards (blue)
5 copies of the $100 bills (green)
1 copy of the $500 bills (green)

Cut apart the cards and bills. Optional: Laminate the cards and bills for durability.

PROCEDURE:

Tell the students:

I will divide the class into six groups. Each group will receive a stack of *Pay Attention Game Cards*. Do not look at the cards until I tell you to do so. Each group will also be assigned a number between one and six. Each group should decide the order in which each person in the group will play. Before I tell you to begin, I will give you one minute to decide the order of the players in your group.

We'll begin with student #1 from Group #1. That person will throw the die and move to the group whose number matches the number on the die. For example, if the die shows a five, the player moves to Group #5.

Then student #1 from Group #5 draws and reads a *Pay Attention Card* to the player who moved to the group. If the leader decides that the moving player's response is correct, he/she is awarded $100, and takes that amount back to his/her original group. If the answer is incorrect, the player returns to his/her original group and no monies are awarded.

A player from Group #2 will then throw the die and move to the group whose number is on the die. Play will then continue as before. As students move to groups, the questions should be asked by group members according to the numerical order they were assigned. The winning group will have the most money at the end of play.

Shuffle the *Pay Attention Cards*. Divide the students into six groups and deal the cards to each group. Begin the game.

(**Note:** In order to have enough $100 bills to play the game, when a team earns five $100 bills they should exchange them for one $500 bill.)

FOLLOW UP:

At the conclusion of the activity, ask the students the following questions:

▸ Which question was the most difficult for you to listen and respond to?
▸ What helped you respond correctly to the mind questions? eyes questions? body language questions? ears questions?

PART

2

**ORGANIZING,
MANAGING TIME,
POSITIVE WORK HABITS,
AND
GOAL-SETTING
STUDY SKILLS**

INTRODUCTION TO ORGANIZING, MANAGING TIME, POSITIVE WORK HABITS, AND GOAL-SETTING STUDY SKILLS

Academic learning develops in coordination with specific developmental study skills. Good basic study skills increase learning, improve school performance and achievement, and enhance positive character traits. If a student can discover even one new thing that helps him/her learn or study better, the areas of learning, achieving, and working will improve as well as his/her quality of life. The activities and games in this section follow four main study skill areas.

First, studying better or more efficiently requires **organizational skills.** These skills include having a comfortable place to study with the necessary materials and without distractions. Another organizational skill is writing down assignments and taking notes on important topics. A commitment of time for studying also leads to an increase in organization and efficiency.

Time management is another study skill which leads to positive academic results. Well-spaced learning sessions instead of "crammed for time" study sessions help enhance retention of material. Also, utilizing the optimum learning time helps the learner become more alert. Review time is very crucial as well, since the more-recent exposure to material leads to better memory skills.

A third study skill is **good work habits**, which complement good study habits and good character development. These good work habits are: being on time to class, turning in assignments on time, beginning work promptly, following directions, sticking to the task at hand (perseverance), listening, and learning the answer to something the student did not know.

The fourth study skill is **motivation** or **goal-setting**. The student needs to set specific study goals as well as education and career goals. If a path is not well defined, the learner will not know if he/she is still on the intended path, has strayed off the path, or has reached the end of the journey.

Continuing self-assessment in the four main developmental study skill areas of organizing, time management, practicing good work habits, and setting goals can lead to higher learning achievement and better self-esteem.

ASCA STANDARDS FOR PART 2

ACADEMIC DEVELOPMENT

Standard A: Students will acquire the attitudes, knowledge and skills that contribute to effective learning in school and across the life span.

A:A1	Improve Academic Self-concept
A:A1.3	Take pride in work and achievement
A:A1.4	Accept mistakes as essential to the learning process
A:A1.5	Identify attitudes and behaviors that lead to successful learning
A:A2	Acquire Skills for Improving Learning
A:A2.1	Apply time-management and task-management skills
A:A2.2	Demonstrate how effort and persistence positively affect learning
A:A2.4	Apply knowledge and learning styles to positively influence school performance
A:A3	Achieve School Success
A:A3.2	Demonstrate the ability to work independently, as well as the ability to work cooperatively with other students
A:A3.5	Share knowledge

Standard B: Students will complete school with the academic preparation essential to choose from a wide range of substantial post- secondary options, including college.

A:B1	Improve Learning
A:B1.2	Learn and apply critical-thinking skills
A:B1.3	Apply the study skills necessary for academic success at each level
A:B1.5	Organize and apply academic information from a variety of sources
A:B1.6	Use knowledge of learning styles to positively influence school performance

Standard C: Students will understand the relationship of academics to the world of work and to life at home and in the community.

A:C1	Relate School To Life Experiences
A:C1.3	Understand the relationship between learning and work

CAREER DEVELOPMENT

Standard A: Students will acquire the skills to investigate the world of work in relation to knowledge of self and to make informed career decisions.

C:A1	Develop Career Awareness
C:A1.4	Learn how to interact and work cooperatively in teams
C:A2	Develop Employment Readiness
C:A2.7	Develop a positive attitude toward work and learning

PERSONAL AND SOCIAL DEVELOPMENT

Standard A: Students will acquire the knowledge, attitudes and interpersonal skills to help them understand and respect self and others.

PS:A1	Acquire Self-Knowledge
PS:A1.3	Learn the goal-setting process
PS:A1.6	Distinguish between appropriate and inappropriate behavior
PS:A1.9	Demonstrate cooperative behavior in groups
PS:A1.10	Identify personal strengths and assets
PS:A2	Acquire Interpersonal Skills
PS:A2.1	Recognize that everyone has rights and responsibilities
PS:A2.2	Respect alternative points of view
PS:A2.6	Use effective communications skills

Standard B: Students will make decisions, set goals and take necessary action to achieve goals.

PS:B1	Self-Knowledge Application
PS:B1.1	Use a decision-making and problem-solving model
PS:B1.3	Identify alternative solutions to a problem

BEACH PARTY COOKOUT
GUIDANCE ACTIVITY

GRADE LEVEL:	3-6
PURPOSE:	To learn why study skills are important
OBJECTIVE:	To make a complete hamburger sandwich with your small group
MATERIALS:	☐ Beach ball or small sponge ball ☐ Dice ☐ *Beach Party Cookout Hamburger Parts* (included on CD) ☐ *Beach Party Cookout* (included on CD)
PRE-LESSON PREPARATION:	Blow up a beach ball or use a small sponge ball. Print *Beach Party Cookout*. Print the following *Beach Party Cookout Hamburger Parts* on medium- or heavy-weight paper: 3 copies of the bun top and bottom 1 copy of the hamburger patty/catsup 1 copy of the tomatoes/pickles/cheese 1 copy of the lettuce Cut out hamburger parts. Optional: Laminate the hamburger part for durability.

PROCEDURE:

Tell the students:

We are going to have a beach party with a cookout. I have a ball to toss around. I'll choose someone to throw the dice. The number on the dice will determine how many passes the whole class will make with the ball before the dice is thrown again. After the dice is thrown, I'll start the game by tossing the ball in the air. Whoever catches it should call out the number "1" and throw the ball back into the air. From then on, whoever catches the ball needs to call out the next number in the sequence, then throw the ball back into

STUDY SKILLS FUN! © 2003 MAR✶CO PRODUCTS, INC. 1-800-448-2197

the air. A student may only catch the ball once during each volley. We can all help by calling the numbers out as a group. The last person will stop the ball when he/she calls out the highest number that was on the dice.

The class will be divided into six groups. It will be the goal of the groups to earn the hamburger parts given for each round by correctly answering questions about study skills. First, the entire class will participate in the beach ball volley. No one may leave his or her seat to volley the ball. You may leave your seat only to return the ball to play. When the volley is completed, each person who caught the ball should stand up. Each group will then select one group member who caught the ball during the volley to represent it and go to the front of the room. Other group members who were part of the volley may help their group representative with the answer. Some groups might not get to come up to the front of the room if no one in the group volleyed the ball for a specific round. Each question will have many answers. When answering the questions, you may not repeat answers that have already been given. Each person who comes up to the front of the room gets only one chance to answer correctly and earn a hamburger part.

We will play eight rounds. The winning group will be the group that has the most "ingredients" on its hamburger.

Divide the class into six groups by having the students count off from 1-6. Begin the game.

FOLLOW-UP:

At the conclusion of the activity, ask the students the following questions:

▶ Which study skills are the most important to you? Why?
▶ Is there a study skill that is most difficult for you? Why is it difficult?

1. **BUN TOP**
2. **PICKLES (3)**
3. **TOMATOES (2)**
4. **CHEESE**
5. **HAMBURGER**
6. **CATSUP**
7. **LETTUCE**
8. **BUN BOTTOM**

A+ BOP
GUIDANCE ACTIVITY

GRADE LEVEL:	2-6
PURPOSE:	To help students become aware of the positive aspects of schoolwork
OBJECTIVE:	To try and become the *A+ Bop It*
MATERIALS:	☐ *A+ Bop Cards* (included on CD) ☐ Soft bopper such as a soft sponge bat ☐ Chair ☐ Chalk
PRE-LESSON PREPARATION:	Print the *A+ Bop Cards* on medium- or heavy-weight paper. Cut out *A+ Bop Cards*. Optional: Laminate the cards for durability.

PROCEDURE:

Draw a chalk line on the floor and place the chair approximately two feet in front of it. Tell the students:

I will choose one person to be *It*. *It* will sit in the chair at the front of the room with his/her back toward the group and hold the soft sponge bat. Each player will draw an *A+ Bop Card* and challenge *It* by standing behind the chair on the chalk line and reading the card aloud. If the card that is read describes a poor study skill, *It* will turn in the chair and make one attempt to tag or bop the player on an appropriate body part. The player can dodge the bop by ducking or leaning back or to one side, but may not move his/her feet. *It* receives credit for an attempted bop. If the card read describes a good study skill, *It* remains still in the chair. If *It* does not bop or bops at the wrong time, *It* looses the A+ position to the player who read the card. After five successes in a row for *It*, a new *It* is chosen. If by chance, *It* bops the player in an inappropriate place, *It* is removed from the game.

Before having the students begin the game, discuss appropriate and inappropriate body parts. It may be helpful to have the leader ask for a volunteer and demonstrate acceptable and unacceptable places for students to be bopped.

Begin the game by choosing one student to be *It* and another to be the first player. Give the first player an *A+ Bop Card* and announce the start of the game. (***Note:*** Cards with statements in **boldface type** describe good study skills.)

FOLLOW-UP:

At the conclusion of the activity, ask the students the following questions:

▸ What helped you most to distinguish a good study skill from a poor study skill?
▸ Which good study skills have you seen your best friend use?

SCHOOL TIME
GUIDANCE ACTIVITY

GRADE LEVEL:	2-6
PURPOSE:	To help students become more aware of their responsibilities in school
OBJECTIVE:	To win points for your team by recognizing good and poor study skills and being the first person to grab a book or bell
MATERIALS:	☐ 2 books or 2 bells ☐ *School Time Statements* (included on CD) ☐ Student desk
PRE-LESSON PREPARATION:	Print the *School Time Statements.*

PROCEDURE:

Place a student desk at the front of the room. Put the two books/bells side by side on the desk. Divide the students into five or six small-group teams. Then tell the students:

I will choose two teams to begin the game. Each team will send one member to the front of the room to stand facing the other team's member. There will be a student desk between them. On the desk are two books/bells, one for each of the two teams represented.

I will read a *School Time Statement* aloud. If what I read is a poor study skill, each player should grab his or her team's book/bell. The first team member to grab its book/bell wins that turn and continues to play the next round. The other player returns to his/her seat and the team sends up another player. If the card describes a good study skill, the players should do nothing. This is considered a draw and each team sends up a new player. That way, more players will get a turn. If a team member mistakenly grabs the book/bell when a good study skill is described, a new team member immediately takes his/her place. A team that wins five turns is declared the winner of the match. Play will then start over with two new teams.

FOLLOW-UP:

At the conclusion of the activity, ask the students the following questions:

▸ Which of these good study skills do you try to practice?
▸ How could any of these poor study skills be improved?

HOP TO IT
GUIDANCE ACTIVITY

GRADE LEVEL: 3-6

PURPOSE: To help students become aware of positive attitudes and actions that enhance learning

OBJECTIVE: To win the most points for your team by being the first person to hop to the schoolbag after his/her number is called

MATERIALS:
☐ 2 schoolbags
☐ *Hop To It Questions* (included on CD)

PRE-LESSON PREPARATION: Print the *Hop To It Questions.*

PROCEDURE:

Tell the students:

I will choose two teams and give each member of each team matching numbers. For example, one person on one team will have the number one, and a person on the other team will also have the number one. Players with matching numbers will be approximately the same distance from the front of the room. I will need to borrow two bookbags from two students and put the bags in the front in the room. Each bag will represent a certain team.

After I ask a *Hop To It Question*, I will randomly call out a number. As soon as you hear your number, hop on one foot to tag the bookbag assigned to your team. The first player to tag his or her team's bookbag and answer the question correctly earns a point for his or her team.

FOLLOW-UP:

At the conclusion of the activity, ask the students the following questions:

▸ Which question was the easiest for you to answer? Why?
▸ Which question was the most difficult for you to answer? Why?

WHAT TIME IS IT WHEN ...
GUIDANCE ACTIVITY

GRADE LEVEL:	2-5
PURPOSE:	To help students become more aware of ways to accept school responsibilities and become more independent
OBJECTIVE:	To earn the most points for your team by drawing a *What Time Is It When… Card* and answering the question correctly
MATERIALS:	☐ *What Time Is It When… Cards* (included on CD) ☐ Dice ☐ Board and chalk/marker
PRE-LESSON PREPARATION:	Print the *What Time Is It When… Cards* on medium- or heavy-weight paper. Cut out the cards. Optional: Laminate the cards for durability.

PROCEDURE:

Tell the students:

I will divide the class into small groups of four or five members. Each group will be identified by a number such as Group #1, Group #2, etc. To begin the game, one member of each small group will come to the front of the room and draw a *What Time Is It When… Card*. If there is a clock on the card and a question, that group member will stay at the front of the room to answer the question. (***Note:*** The answers to the questions are not a certain time of the day, but the procedure that should take place when the incident occurs. For example: What time of the morning is it when your alarm clock goes off? Answer: Time to get out of bed and get ready for the day.) If the picture on the card shows a sleeping (ZZZZZ) person and there is no question, the student who drew the card will go back to his or her small group and will not have a chance to earn points during that round.

After it has been determined which small group members will remain at the front of the room to answer questions, each student will take a turn reading his or her card's question and answering it out loud. If the answer is correct, the group representative throws the dice to determine the number of points that the correct answer earned. If the answer is

 STUDY SKILLS FUN! © 2003 MAR★CO PRODUCTS, INC. 1-800-448-2197

incorrect, the representative from the next numerical group is given a chance to answer the question for five extra points. For example, if the representative for Group #2 answers incorrectly, the representative from Group #3 is given the chance to earn extra points. Each team's points will be recorded on the board.

After each representative has had a turn answering the question on a card, the students return to their respective groups and a new player from each group comes to the front of the room. Continue the procedure until all group members have had a turn. The winning group is the one that has the most points after everyone has had a turn.

FOLLOW-UP:

At the conclusion of the activity, ask the students the following questions:

▸ What was one question on the *What Time Is It When… Cards* that you believe would be good to ask yourself?
▸ Which question do you think your friend does best?

BALLOON-LANDING
GUIDANCE ACTIVITY

GRADE LEVEL: 3-6

PURPOSE: To encourage students to understand and instantly recognize many ways to achieve good study skills

OBJECTIVE: To respond to open-ended study skill questions with many different answers before a tossed balloon hits the ground

MATERIALS:
- ☐ 1 balloon
- ☐ *Balloon-Landing Questions* (included on CD)
- ☐ *Hit Cards* (included on CD)
- ☐ Die
- ☐ Board and chalk/marker

PRE-LESSON PREPARATION: Blow up the balloon, and tie a knot in the end.

Print the *Balloon-Landing Questions*.

Print the *Hit Cards* on medium- or heavy-weight paper. Cut out the cards. Optional: Laminate the cards for durability.

PROCEDURE:

Tell the students:

I will divide the class into small groups of five to six members. Each group will take a turn answering a study skill question. Each question has a lot of different answers that you can call out. When it is your turn, your group will come to the front the room and stand in a circle. I will read one of the questions from the *Balloon-Landing Questions*. A member of the group will then throw the die to see how many answers must be given before the balloon lands on the ground.

I will choose someone from another team to toss the balloon up in the middle of the playing team's circle. The playing team can then begin calling out answers. Each correct answer earns a point for the team. When answering the questions, you may not repeat answers that have already been given. The object is for the playing team to call out at least as

 STUDY SKILLS FUN! © 2003 MAR✶CO PRODUCTS, INC. 1-800-448-2197

many answers as the number on the die before the balloon lands on the ground, a chair, a desk, or a team member. During this time, no team member may hit the balloon. If a team member hits the balloon, his or her team must sit down, and wait for its next turn. The team will not earn points during a round when a member hits the balloon.

A team that calls out more answers than the number on the die before the balloon lands earns one *Hit Card* for each allowable extra answer. These *Hit Cards* can be used to push the balloon up again during a toss. For example, if a team gives two extra answers to the *Balloon-Landing Question* before the balloon lands, the team will earn two *Hit Cards*, which can be used to push the balloon back up in the air the next time that team takes a turn. Each team's points will be recorded on the board at the end of its turn. The winning team is the one with the most points when all of the questions have been answered.

FOLLOW-UP:

At the conclusion of the activity, ask the students the following questions:

▸ Which question was the easiest to answer?
▸ Which question was the most difficult to answer? Why?

STUDYING HORSE FEATHERS
GUIDANCE ACTIVITY

GRADE LEVEL:	3-6
PURPOSE:	To help students set studying goals
OBJECTIVE:	To blow the group's feather toward a good study skill goal and get rid of the circle goals by correctly answering questions
MATERIALS:	☐ *Studying Horse Feathers Statements* (included on CD) ☐ *Colored Circles* (included on CD) ☐ Small feathers as from a feather duster or craft store ☐ Scissors ☐ Die ☐ Optional: Tape
PRE-LESSON PREPARATION:	Collect feathers. Print the *Studying Horse Feathers Statements* and, on medium- or heavy-weight paper,

1 copy of the red circles
1 copy of the purple circles
1 copy of the orange circles
1 copy of the green circles
1 copy of the blue circles
1 copy of the yellow circles
6 copies of the white circles

Cut out either the circles or, to save time, the squares framing each circle. Optional: Laminate the circles for durability.

PROCEDURE:

Tell the students:

Some people might think that study skills are just a bunch of "horse feathers" or, in other words, unimportant. But we're going to prove today that study skills are very important in helping you do better in school and in life.

I will divide the class into six small groups. Each group is to sit around a table or desk. Each group will have a set of six differently colored circles. Each circle has a number and represents a different study skill.

STUDY SKILLS FUN! © 2003 MAR✶CO PRODUCTS, INC. 1-800-448-2197

The numbers, colors, and study skills are:

#1, red, organization	(1 red circle to each small group)
#2, purple, time management	(1 purple circle to each small group)
#3, orange, goal-setting	(1 orange circle to each small group)
#4, green, following directions	(1 green circle to each small group)
#5, blue, listening	(1 blue circle to each small group)
#6, yellow, attitude	(1 yellow circle to each small group)

(6 white circles, numbered 1-6, to each small group)

The circles are to be spread around your group's table or desk. (Optional: If you printed the circles on lighter-weight paper, use a small circle of tape to hold the circles in place when the students blow on the feathers.) Each group will also have a horse feather which must be blown toward the good study skill goal represented by a colored circle. The feather is placed in front of the person taking his or her turn and no one else may blow the feather during that person's turn.

I will choose one person at random to throw the die. The number on the die will tell the selected group member which circle to blow the feather toward. I will tell you which study skill goal the numbered circle represents. It is important that you remember the study skill, because this is the only time you will hear it. When I say, "Go," the person selected for each group will blow the horse feather toward the identified circle. Other group members may encourage the player to meet the challenge, but they must not blow. If the feather lands on the floor, any group member may place it back in front of the person who was blowing it and he or she may begin again. The first person to have at least one third of his/her feather in the correct circle calls out, "Horse feathers!"

I will then read one statement from the *Studying Horse Feathers Statements*. The person calling out "Horse feathers!" must then explain why the statement describes a good study skill. If the answer is correct, and not a repetition of something that has been said previously, the group may take the colored circle, place it to the side, and count it as one point for the team. The white circle with the same number as the removed color circle should then be placed in the empty spot.

Each group will then select another player and the game will continue. If the needed colored circle has been removed and used as a point, the white circle is used in its place. A player who reaches the white circle, calls out, "Horse feathers!" and is able to give a correct answer earns a point for his or her team.

The game ends when each player in the group has had a turn to blow the feather. The group with the most points at the end of the game wins the game.

FOLLOW-UP:

At the conclusion of the activity, ask the students the following questions:

▸ Which goal do you think you would like to work on this week? Why?
▸ Which goal would help you improve your grades? Why?

ROADBLOCKS
GUIDANCE ACTIVITY

GRADE LEVEL:	2-6
PURPOSE:	To help students become aware of situations that can prevent someone from having good study skills
OBJECTIVE:	To avoid being caught in a roadblock and to continue being the undefeated *Dog*
MATERIALS:	☐ *Roadblock Cards* (included on CD)
PRE-LESSON PREPARATION:	Print the *Roadblock Cards* on medium- or heavy-weight paper. Cut out the cards. Optional: Laminate the cards for durability.

PROCEDURE:

Tell the students:

This is a game played by two characters, Cat and Dog. I will choose one person to be the Cat and another person to be the Dog. By walking only, the Dog is to try and tag the Cat, who is also walking to get away. If either the Dog or Cat is running in the room, that player sits down, and another person takes his or her place.

The rest of the students will remain seated and try to protect the Cat from being caught by the Dog. For example, if the Dog gets too close to the Cat, the Cat can quickly tag any seated player to take his or her place. This is done as quickly as possible, with the hope that the Dog does not see the tag taking place. The newly tagged person is now the Cat and begins walking to keep away from the Dog. The previous Cat continues walking back to his or her original seat. If the Dog does not see the tag take place he or she will continue chasing the original Cat. This gives the new Cat time to keep away from the Dog. This is why the tag should be made as quickly as possible.

If the Dog catches the Cat, the Cat will read a *Roadblock Card*. If the card describes a good study skill, the same person continues to be the Dog and the Cat chooses a person who is seated to be the next Cat. If the *Roadblock Card* describes a poor study skill, the Cat becomes the Dog and the Dog chooses a person who is seated to be the next Cat.

 STUDY SKILLS FUN! © 2003 MAR∗CO PRODUCTS, INC. 1-800-448-2197

If the Dog doesn't catch the Cat after one to two minutes, stop the chase and let the Dog read a *Roadblock Card*. If the study skill described is a good one, the Cat gets to be the Dog. If the study skill described is a poor one, the Cat chooses a person who is seated to be the next Cat and the Dog chooses a seated person to be the next Dog.

FOLLOW-UP:

At the conclusion of the activity, ask the students the following questions:

▸ Which *Roadblock Card* was one that you need to improve upon?
▸ What is the best way to improve study skills?

SHAPE-UP OLYMPIC CHALLENGES
GUIDANCE ACTIVITY

GRADE LEVEL:	4-6
PURPOSE:	To learn and practice study techniques that improve memory
OBJECTIVE:	To earn as many *Shape-Up Tickets* as possible

MATERIALS:

- [ ] *Shape-Up Olympic Challenges* (pages 58-67)
- [ ] *Shape-Up Tickets* (included on CD)
- [ ] *Fold And Check* (for *Fold And Check Challenge*, included on CD)
- [ ] Scratch paper
- [ ] Pencils
- [ ] Board and chalk or chart paper and marker

PRE-LESSON PREPARATION: Print two copies of the *Shape-Up Tickets* on medium- or heavy-weight paper. Cut out the tickets. Optional: Laminate the tickets for durability.

PROCEDURE:

Each *Shape-Up Olympic Challenge Competition* will take one session to complete.

Tell the students:

I will divide everyone in the group into two permanent teams for the *Shape-Up Olympic Challenges*. I will then give each member of each team a permanent number between one and the number of students in the group. This means that each player on each team will have the same number as a player on the opposite team. (If the number of team members is uneven, add the following sentence.) Some team members will have more than one number so that every player's number will match the number of a player on the opposite team.

After deciding which team will go first, I will read a *Shape-Up Olympic Challenge* activity aloud to both teams. The teams will take turns as long as the activity is being performed correctly. If someone makes an error, his or her team's turn is over. The other team continues to play until every team member has participated or someone makes an error.

 STUDY SKILLS FUN! © 2003 MAR∗CO PRODUCTS, INC. 1-800-448-2197

A *Shape-Up Ticket* will be earned each time the activity is performed correctly. This means if every person on a team performs the activity correctly, the team can earn as many *Shape-Up Tickets* as there are students on the team. At the end of each round, I will collect the *Shape-Up Tickets* and record the number of each team's points on the board/chart paper. It will be all right if some answers are given more than once, because repetition is a good study skill and this provides you with more practice in developing it.

The *Shape-Up Olympic Challenges* will provide you with ideas and practice in learning and remembering material you have been assigned to study. Concentrate on each activity as you perform it, and discover which ideas would help you most in learning new material. You may write down those ideas on a piece of scratch paper.

The winning team will have earned the most *Shape-Up Tickets* for that particular challenge. The *Shape-Up Olympic Challenge* Champion Team will be the team that wins the most challenges.

Tell the students to take out a piece of paper and a pencil. Explain that throughout the challenges, they may want to make notes about the ideas presented for future reference. Divide the students into two permanent teams, assign a permanent number to each team member, and begin the first challenge. After each challenge, collect the *Shape-Up Tickets*, record each team's total, then write the name of the winning team on the board/chart paper.

FOLLOW-UP:

After each challenge, ask the students the following questions:

▸ How did this activity help you learn something new?
▸ How can you use this learning skill in school? Away from school?
▸ Was this an idea you wanted to write on your scratch paper?

SHAPE-UP OLYMPIC CHALLENGE—VISUAL LEARNING

Refer to pages 56-57 for directions. Then tell the students:

Before our competition begins, we will practice a way to learn or memorize material through visual clues. To do this, you must link what you want to learn with a word you picture in your mind. For example, you may link what you want to remember with a rhyming word such as: one-bun; two-shoe; three-tree; four-door; five-hive; six-sticks; seven-oven; eight-gate; nine-line; ten-hen. Repeat these picture words with me. (Repeat with the whole group once or more.) Now who can say all of these alone? (Call on volunteers.)

Now try to remember these ten grocery items in order by seeing each item in a picture. One-bun-milk: Picture the bun being dunked into a glass of milk. Two-shoe-lettuce: Picture lettuce coming out of a shoe. Three-tree-bread: What can we picture for this? (Allow time for students' suggestions.) Pick one of the suggestions you have just heard and picture it in your mind. Four-door-lunchmeat. I'm going to let you make up your own pictures for the rest of the items. I will name them, then pause in order for you to think of a picture in your mind. (Name six more grocery items, stopping every so often to check whether anyone can rename all of the items named so far. Let the students continue to share the pictures they are imagining for some of the items.)

This is called visual learning. You've practiced visual learning by linking the words you want to learn with pictures in your mind. Now we will begin our *Shape-Up Olympic Challenge Competition*. Each team member has already been assigned a number. I will call on each team, beginning with number _____. (Begin with any number you choose.) I will switch back and forth between the two teams. We will begin by reciting the entire list of grocery items we have just practiced. Think about the picture you linked with each item in your mind and name only the grocery items aloud. If a team member misses the list order, the other team has a chance to earn extra tickets by letting team members repeat the list order. At times, I may ask you to share the visual picture you had for remembering an item.

When the students have finished reciting the list, continue the challenge, using the lists below or other lists appropriate for the class. You may write the lists on the board/chart paper for everyone to see until everyone has memorized them. Then remove the list and begin the *Shape-Up Olympic Challenge Competition*.

Extra lists for visual learning:

▶ ham, hot dogs, catsup, beans, corn, apples, oranges, soap, paper plates, ice cream
▶ football, basketball, soccer, baseball, weightlifting, swimming, running, ice hockey, boxing, wrestling

At the conclusion of the activity, ask the students the following questions:

▶ How did this activity help you learn something new?
▶ How can you use this learning skill in school? Away from school?
▶ Was this an idea you wanted to write on your scratch paper?

STUDY SKILLS FUN! © 2003 MAR∗CO PRODUCTS, INC. 1-800-448-2197

SHAPE-UP OLYMPIC CHALLENGE—USING YOUR SENSES

Refer to pages 56-57 for directions. Then write the word *Mississippi* on the board/chart paper. Tell the students:

> We are going to learn to spell the word Mississippi using the senses of seeing, touching, and hearing. These are the steps that we will use: (Practice the following steps with the entire class.)
>
> 1. Look at the word. (seeing)
> 2. Write the word with your finger on your desk or write it on paper with your pencil. Do this three times. If you are still not sure you know how to spell the word, continue writing it until you are sure. (touching)
> 3. Quietly say the word out loud and spell it out loud to yourself. (hearing)

Ask for volunteers to spell the word out loud to the class. Then continue speaking to the class:

> The *Shape-Up Olympic Challenge Competition* will begin now. I will write a word on the board/chart paper and give you time to follow the three steps we have just completed. Then I will erase the word and begin switching back and forth between the two teams, asking each team member to spell the same word. If a team member misspells the word, I will continue with the other team until a member of that team misspells the word. Each team member who spells the word correctly will earn a *Shape-Up Ticket*. Be sure to learn the words by following the three steps we just practiced.

Use any words that the class is working on or the following suggested extra words:

▸ calm, recent, bamboo, romance, jungle, promptly, figure, number, opposite, single, comet, realize, settlement, comfort

At the conclusion of the activity, ask the students the following questions:

▸ How did this activity help you learn something new?
▸ How can you use this learning skill in school? Away from school?
▸ Was this an idea you wanted to write on your scratch paper?

SHAPE-UP OLYMPIC CHALLENGE—FOLD AND CHECK

Refer to pages 56-57 for directions. Give each student a copy of *Fold And Check,* a piece of paper*,* and a pencil. Have a copy of *Fold And Check* and pencil for yourself, so that you can show the students what to do while you are giving them directions. Then tell the students:

Fold the sheet of blank paper the long way. Keep the fold on the right side of the paper. Keep the paper folded. When we begin, I will write a word on the board/chart paper. You will be given some time to study the word and write it on your paper. Then I will erase the word and you will turn your paper over. The fold will then be on the left side of the paper. You will then write the word from memory. When you have done this, open your paper and check to see if you spelled the word correctly. Once you have written the word, you may not change the spelling until I have seen your work.

Before we start, let's practice to make sure everyone is clear on what to do. Turn your paper so the fold is on the right side. The word I want you to write is *noise*. (Write the word on the board/chart paper.) Write it on your paper and look at it. (Pause for about 30 seconds.) Now I will erase the word. (Erase the word.) Turn your paper over so the fold is on the left side. Write the word *noise*, then open your paper and check your work. Raise your hand if you spelled the word *noise* correctly.

Now we will begin the *Shape-Up Olympic Challenge Competition*. I will give you the word to spell by saying it and writing it on the board. (Write the word.) Copy the word onto the top side of your *Fold And Check* paper. Be sure the fold is on the right side. Study the word as I erase it from the board. You may want to use the three steps you learned in the *Using Your Senses* exercise. Turn over your paper. The fold is now on the left. Write the word as you remember it. (Pause for the students to follow your directions.) Put your pencils down. I will call on the person who is number ___ on one team to start by coming up to me and showing me the word written from memory on his or her *Fold And Check* paper. If the word is spelled correctly, the team member will earn a *Shape-Up Ticket*. I will then check the paper of each member of that team and award a ticket to each person with the correct answer, until some one has misspelled the word. If the word is spelled incorrectly, the opposite team member with the corresponding number will show me what he or she has written from memory. If it is spelled incorrectly, the team's turn is over. However, if it is spelled correctly the team member will earn a ticket. I will then check the other team members' papers, awarding a ticket to each person with a correct answer. A team's turn will end when every team member has been given a ticket or when I find a team member with a misspelled word. Remember, if a team member has spelled the word incorrectly, that team's turn is over, whether or not other team members have the word spelled correctly.

Use any words the class needs to learn such as those from the science, social studies, math, or spelling curriculum. Or use the following suggested words:

▸ moment, cosmic, friendship, denominator, multiplication, reverse, receive, problem

Begin the activity by stating and writing the first word.

At the conclusion of the activity, ask the students the following questions:

▸ How did this activity help you learn something new?
▸ How can you use this learning skill in school? Away from school?
▸ Was this an idea you wanted to write on your scratch paper?

 STUDY SKILLS FUN! © 2003 MAR∗CO PRODUCTS, INC. 1-800-448-2197

SHAPE-UP OLYMPIC CHALLENGE—MNEMONIC DEVICE

Refer to pages 56-57 for directions. Then tell the students:

One way to remember a list of words is to make a sentence using the first letter of each word in the list. For example, learning this sentence would help you know the order of the nine planets: My very eager mother just served us nine pizzas. Once you know the sentence, think of the first letter of each word. Instead of saying that word in the sentence, say the name of the planet: M-Mercury (My); V-Venus (very); E-Earth (eager); M-Mars (mother); J-Jupiter (just); S-Saturn (served); U-Uranus (us); N-Neptune (nine); P-Pluto (pizzas).

I'm going to give you a few minutes to practice this quietly on your own. (Pause for a limited amount of time.) Who will volunteer to name all nine planets in order? (Allow two volunteers to recite the names of the planets.)

Now we are ready to begin the *Shape-Up Olympic Challenge Competition*. I will call on the team members beginning with number _____ and switch back and forth between the two teams for correct answers. I will give you a *Shape-Up Ticket* for each correct answer. If any answer is incorrect, the other team will have a chance to earn an extra ticket every time a team member answers a question correctly.

Now, beginning with number _____, name the nine planets in order. You may say the sentence to yourself to help you remember.

(**Note:** If the class already knows the names of the planets, you may substitute any appropriate list. For example, you might have the students learn the names of the bones of the leg: femur [thigh], tibia and fibula [calf], patella [knee cap]. Tell the students to learn these in order. Write the words on the board and have the students work alone or with a partner on their team to make up their own sentence.)

Extra lists for practicing this memory technique:

▸ Name the seven dwarfs in *Snow White* in order: Sleepy, Dopey, Sneezy, Doc, Grumpy, Happy, and Bashful.
▸ Name the 13 original colonies in order: Delaware, Pennsylvania, New Jersey, Georgia, Connecticut, Massachusetts, Maryland, South Carolina, New Hampshire, Virginia, New York, North Carolina, Rhode Island.
▸ Name the continents: Asia, Africa, North America, South America, Australia, Antarctica, Europe
▸ Use any curriculum list the class is working on.

At the conclusion of the activity, ask the students the following questions:

▸ How did this activity help you learn something new?
▸ How can you use this learning skill in school? Away from school?
▸ Was this an idea you wanted to write on your scratch paper?

SHAPE-UP OLYMPIC CHALLENGE—MAKE UP A SONG

Refer to pages 56-57 for directions. Then tell the students:

> In this study skills challenge, we will make up words to a familiar song in order to memorize items. To learn the parts of a plant, for example, we will use the song *I'm A Little Teapot*. Instead of singing the actual words, we will sing, "I'm a little rose plant, tall and slim. Here is my root system, here is my stem. When I get all bloomed out, then you view my leaf, bud, and petal stigma, too." Practice this with someone close to you on your team. (Pause for a limited time.) Are there two volunteers who can sing the song together? (Let the volunteers demonstrate or let the whole group sing together.)
>
> Now we will begin the *Shape-Up Olympic Challenge Competition*. I will call on number _____, and that team member will tell me the parts of a plant. You need only sing the song in your mind to help you remember the names of the parts. We will switch back and forth between the two teams for correct answers. I will give you a *Shape-Up Ticket* if you can name the parts of a plant. If any answer is incorrect, the other team will have a chance to earn an extra ticket every time a team member correctly names the parts of a plant.

Begin the activity by starting with the number selected when giving directions to the students. Continue the activity by providing extra lists and letting each team member work closely with another team member, picking their own song.

Suggested lists to learn:

▸ Name the five greatest oceans on earth: Pacific, Atlantic, Indian, Arctic, Antarctic.
▸ Name 10 mammals: (students' choice).
▸ Name the first five Presidents of the United States: George Washington, John Adams, Thomas Jefferson, James Madison, James Monroe

At the conclusion of the activity, ask the students the following questions:

▸ How did this activity help you learn something new?
▸ How can you use this learning skill in school? Away from school?
▸ Was this an idea you wanted to write on your scratch paper?

SHAPE-UP OLYMPIC CHALLENGE—DRAW IT

Refer to pages 56-57 for directions. Distribute paper and a pencil to each student. Then say:

In this study skills challenge, we will learn to remember a word's definition by drawing a picture of it. Let's try the word constitution. *A constitution* is *a document that describes the fundamental rules or laws by which a nation, state, or group is governed.* Now I need two volunteers to draw a picture of this word's definition on the board. (If necessary, suggest drawing something to represent an important paper or a law. Have the volunteers draw their pictures on the board.) Now tell us the definition of the word constitution by describing what you see in the picture. You don't need to give the definition exactly as I gave it. Just include the main idea. (Pause for answers from the group.)

We will now begin the *Shape-Up Olympic Challenge Competition.* I will give you a word and repeat the definition as many times as necessary or write it on the board. Then I will give you a few minutes to draw a picture of this definition at your desk and to think about how to explain your drawing. Your definition does not have to be stated in the words I give, but it has to express the same idea.

I will begin by calling on number _____ from both teams, then switch back and forth between the two teams. Each team will earn a *Shape-Up Ticket* for each correct answer. If any team member gives an incorrect answer, the other team can continue to earn *Shape-Up Tickets* as long as its members give correct answers. When giving your answer, you may share the picture you drew to help you remember the definition.

Here is the first definition. Listen and draw a picture of it. The word is *accelerate*. Its definition is: *to move faster.*

Give the students time to draw their pictures of the definition. Then begin the activity by starting with the number selected when giving directions to the students. Continue the activity for as long as time allows.

Extra suggested words:

▸ Evaporate: to give off moisture, such as fog off of a lake
▸ Indicate: to point out something, such as a sign.
▸ Pandemonium: an uproar, lawlessness
▸ Construct: to build something; to put something together
▸ Any curriculum vocabulary the students need to learn

At the conclusion of the activity, ask the students the following questions:

▸ How did this activity help you learn something new?
▸ How can you use this learning skill in school? Away from school?
▸ Was this an idea you wanted to write on your scratch paper?

SHAPE-UP OLYMPIC CHALLENGE—SQR3: SURVEY

Refer to pages 56-57 for directions. Then tell the students:

The first part of the study skill *SQR3* (Survey, Question, Read, Recite, Review) is *Survey*. That is what we will practice first. When you are going to read something, you do several things before you begin. You may look for pictures, graphs, captions, tables, or other clues that tell you what the chapter is about. Take out your (science, social studies, math, etc.) book. Survey chapter _____ on page _____ by looking at the things that will give you clues about the text. (Pause for a limited time.) Who can tell me one thing that will be a subject of this chapter? (Pause for answers.)

Now we will begin the *Shape-Up Olympic Challenge Competition*. (If necessary, remind the students who is on which team and what number has been assigned to each student.) I will call out a team number and ask the person who was assigned that number to name one thing the chapter will be about. Then I will call on the person with the same number on the opposite team. From then on, I will switch back and forth between the two teams, awarding *Shape-Up Tickets* to each team member giving a correct answer. In this activity, you cannot repeat anything that has already been said. You must name something different. When I think that we have covered most of the items in the chapter, we will go on to another chapter.

Now that you know what we are going to do, we will begin with another chapter. Use your (science, social studies, math, etc.) book and survey chapter _____ on page _____. In a few minutes, I will begin with number _____. Remember, each of you is to name only one thing about the chapter and no answer can repeat another person's answer.

At the conclusion of the activity, ask the students the following questions:

▸ How did this activity help you learn something new?
▸ How can you use this learning skill in school? Away from school?
▸ Was this an idea you wanted to write on your scratch paper?

SHAPE-UP OLYMPIC CHALLENGE—SQR3: QUESTION

Refer to pages 56-57 for directions. Then tell the students:

We have completed *Survey*, the first part of the *SQR3* study skill. Today we are going to learn more of the *SQR3* study skill by practicing the second part, *Question*. For this activity, we will practice how to form questions about any reading assignment before actually reading it. Doing this will help us recognize what information to look for as we read.

Take out your (science, social studies, math, etc.) book. Turn to chapter _____ on page _____. Look at the headings in bold print above the sections to be read. We are going to practice turning these headings into questions whose answers can be found by reading the material. For example, if the heading says, *Parts Of A Plant*, the question could be, "What are the parts of a plant?" Take a few minutes to look at the different headings in this chapter. (Pause for a limited time.) Now let's look at the first bold heading in the chapter. Who can turn that heading into a question so that we will know what to look for when we read that section? (Allow two students to answer the question.)

Now we are ready to begin the *Shape-Up Olympic Challenge Competition*. I will call on the team member assigned number _____ and ask him or her to turn the next heading into a question. I will switch back and forth between the two teams moving from one heading to another and awarding *Shape-Up Tickets* to each team member giving a correct answer. In this activity, you cannot repeat any answer that has already been used. You must give a different answer.

Begin the activity. When the students have finished with one chapter, go on to other chapters for as long as time allows.

At the conclusion of the activity, ask the students the following questions:

▸ How did this activity help you learn something new?
▸ How can you use this learning skill in school? Away from school?
▸ Was this an idea you wanted to write on your scratch paper?

SHAPE-UP OLYMPIC CHALLENGE— SQR3: READ AND RECITE

Refer to pages 56-57 for directions. Then tell the students:

SQR3 is a study skill that stands for *Survey, Question, Read, Recite*, and *Review*. We have practiced *Survey* and *Question*. Today we will practice *Read* and *Recite*. Later we will do *Review*. Take out your (science, social studies, math, etc.) book and turn to chapter _____ on page _____. Look at the first bold heading. Be sure to turn that heading into a question, as we have already learned to do. Now read the first paragraph. Recite to yourself, in your own words, what that paragraph was about and be prepared to share your answer with the group. (Pause while you and the students read the paragraph.) Who can tell us what the paragraph was about? (Allow two students to answer.)

Now we will begin the *Shape-Up Olympic Challenge Competition*. (If necessary, remind the students who is on which team and what number has been assigned to each student.) Read the next paragraph, and look up at me when you have finished. I will begin with number _____ on team _____, asking that person to recite the main ideas of the paragraph. If the answer is correct, that person's team will earn a *Shape-Up Ticket*. If his or her answer is wrong, I will go to the other team and ask the person with the same number to answer the question. I will switch back and forth until someone answers the question correctly. That player's team will earn a *Shape-Up Ticket*. You will then read the next paragraph, and we will repeat the process with the team that did not begin the last round having the first opportunity to answer the question.

Begin the activity, working through the designated chapter. If time allows, go on to another chapter.

At the conclusion of the activity, ask the students the following questions:

▸ How did this activity help you learn something new?
▸ How can you use this learning skill in school? Away from school?
▸ Was this an idea you wanted to write on your scratch paper?

STUDY SKILLS FUN! © 2003 MAR✶CO PRODUCTS, INC. 1-800-448-2197

SHAPE-UP OLYMPIC CHALLENGE—SQR3: REVIEW

Refer to pages 56-57 for directions. Then tell the students:

Now we are going to practice the third R, *Review*, in the study skill *SQR3*. We will go back to a chapter that we read during the *Read* and *Recite* part of study skill *SQR3*. Take out your (science, social studies, math, etc.) book and turn to chapter _____ on page _____. We will review by going back over the bold headings from the previous session, turning the headings into questions, and seeing if we can answer the questions about the section. If you are unable to answer the question based on the bold heading, you will need to reread the section.

Now we will begin the *Shape-Up Olympic Challenge Competition*. (If necessary, remind the students who is on which team and what number has been assigned to each student.) I will turn the first bold heading into a question. Then I will begin the activity by calling on number _____ from team _____ to answer the question. If the answer is correct, I will award that player's team a *Shape-Up Ticket* and continue by turning the next bold heading into a question and calling on number _____ from the opposite team. If that player's answer is incorrect, I will call on the member of the opposite team who has the matching number and ask him or her to answer the question. I will continue switching back and forth until someone gives a correct answer. That player's team will be awarded a *Shape-Up Ticket*. I will continue through the chapter, switching back and forth between the teams, asking questions based on the bold headings, and awarding *Shape-Up Tickets*. The team with the most *Shape-Up Tickets* when our time is up is the winner.

At the conclusion of the activity, ask the students the following questions:

▸ How did this activity help you learn something new?
▸ How can you use this learning skill in school? Away from school?
▸ Was this an idea you wanted to write on your scratch paper?

DODGE CITY STUDY SKILLS
GUIDANCE ACTIVITY

GRADE LEVEL: 2-6

PURPOSE: To learn to recognize better choices in studying

OBJECTIVE: To earn *Key To The City Cards* by answering open-ended questions and by staying up front the longest without being hit by the sponge ball

MATERIALS:
- ☐ *Dodge City Incomplete Sentences* (included on CD)
- ☐ *Key To The City Cards* (included on CD)
- ☐ Small sponge ball

PRE-LESSON PREPARATION: Print the *Dodge City Incomplete Sentences*.

Print the *Key To The City Cards* on medium- or heavy-weight paper. Cut out cards. Optional: Laminate the cards for durability.

PROCEDURE:

Tell the students:

How many of you have ever played dodgeball? You know that the object of the game is not to let the ball hit you. In other words, you avoid being hit by the ball. Sometimes students avoid doing their homework, don't listen in class, don't pay attention, or do lots of other things that are not good study skills. Today's lesson is going to be about dodging.

First, I will choose six to eight players to line up across the wall in the front of the room. Each player will be asked to complete a *Dodge City Incomplete Sentence*. I will read the first part of the sentence and each player will complete that sentence. Once an answer has been given, it cannot be repeated. Each incomplete sentence includes the word dodge so it is important to listen carefully and give an answer that tells what happens if you dodge or avoid doing something or what happens if you do not dodge or avoid doing something. The players who complete sentences correctly may stay at the front of the room. A player whose answer is incorrect, must return to his or her seat.

Next, I will choose three students to come to the front of the room and throw the sponge ball at the players lined up along the wall. The throwers should stand at least five feet from the lined-up players. Each person will have one chance to try to do this and the thrower will be disqualified if the ball is not aimed at an appropriate place on the person's body. The players at the front of the room may move from side to side to avoid the ball but must remain standing against the wall. A player who is hit must sit down.

After the ball has been thrown, the players remaining at the front of the room receive a *Key To The City Card* and remain in place for the next round. New players will replace those who had to sit down. You will repeat the same procedure until I tell you time is up.

Whoever has the most *Key To The City Cards* wins the game.

Tell the students the parts of the body that are appropriate to hit with the ball: arms, legs, shoulder, etc. Then choose players and begin the activity.

FOLLOW-UP:

At the conclusion of the activity, ask the students the following questions:

- ▸ Which question referred to a study skill that you use?
- ▸ Which *Dodge City Incomplete Sentence* was the most difficult for you to complete? Why?

HOLE IN ONE
GUIDANCE ACTIVITY

GRADE LEVEL:	3-6
PURPOSE:	To review good study skills
OBJECTIVE:	To earn the most points for your group by rolling a golf ball into cups marked with points and distinguishing good study skills from poor study skills
MATERIALS:	☐ 2 golf balls ☐ 6-8 large-sized styrofoam or plastic cups with points—such as 10, 20, 30, etc.—marked with a marker on the bottom of each cup ☐ *Hole-In-One Cards* (included on CD) ☐ 2 golf clubs (optional) ☐ Chalk and tape measure
PRE-LESSON PREPARATION:	Label the cups with their point values. Print the *Hole-In-One Cards* on medium- or heavy-weight paper. Cut out the cards. Optional: Laminate the cards for durability.

PROCEDURE:

(**Note:** This activity should be presented after the students have participated in the *Shape-Up Olympic Challenge Competition. Hole-In-One Cards* with an [*] relate to something taught in the *Competition.*)

Place the cups on their sides and line them up so that the bottom of each cup is against the wall. Draw a chalk line six feet from the cups. Tell the students:

I will divide the class into two teams. One member of each team will come to the front of the room at the same time. Each player will stand at the chalk line and try to put his or her golf ball into any of the cups. (**Note:** Give directions for either rolling the ball or using the golf clubs.) A point value is marked on the bottom of each cup. I've mixed up the cups, so the points aren't in order. During the game, I will also be moving the cups around to different positions.

STUDY SKILLS FUN! © 2003 MAR*CO PRODUCTS, INC. 1-800-448-2197

If your ball goes into one of the cups, look on the bottom of the cup to see its point value. Then take a *Hole-In-One Card* and read it out loud.

If your card describes a good study skill, your team earns the number of points written on the cup.

If your card describes a skill related to studying, and you correctly complete the skill, your team earns the number of points written on the cup.

If your card describes a study skill that is not good, your team earns no points unless you can make a suggestion about how to turn the poor study skill into a good study skill.

If your ball does not go into one of the cups, take a *Hole-In-One Card*, read it out loud, and answer it. You may earn one point by correctly answering the card, but no additional points.

The game ends when each player on both teams has had a turn at rolling/hitting the golf ball. The team with the most points at the end of the game wins the game.

FOLLOW-UP:

At the conclusion of the activity, ask the students the following questions:

▸ Which good study skill have you seen someone in this room using? Who was using that good study skill?
▸ Which poor study skill would be easiest to change into a good study skill?

INSTRUCTIONS FOR USING THE CD

The CD found inside the back cover provides ADOBE® PDF files of each of the activities reproducible game cards and activity sheets.

Most of the PDFs may be printed in color or black and white. Choose the appropriate setting on your computer. You may also chose to print some of the cards on color paper instead of printing them in color,

These files cannot be modified/edited.

System requirements to open PDF (.pdf) files:

Adobe Reader® 5.0 or newer (compatible with Windows 2000® or newer or Mac OS 9.0® or newer).

We suggest you print a copy of each reproducible page and save them with the leader's guide in case the CD is lost or damaged.

> ## THIS CD MAY NOT BE DUPLICATED OR DISTRIBUTED.

PERMISSION TO REPRODUCE: The purchaser may reproduce the activity sheets, free and without special permission, for participant use for a particular group or class. Sharing these files with other counselors/faculty members or reproduction of these materials for an entire school system is forbidden.